MAKE YOUR OWN FURNITURE

HOW TO DO IT
THE FUN AND EASY WAY

MAKE YOUR OWN FURNITURE

HOW TO DO IT
THE FUN AND EASY WAY

PAUL HOWARD
Illustrated by J. Hodgkinson
Edited by Fiona McCall

Pagurian Press

DUTTON

Copyright © 1978 PAGURIAN PRESS LIMITED
Suite 1106, 335 Bay Street, Toronto, Ontario, Canada

A Christopher Ondaatje Publication. Copyright under the Berne Convention. All rights reserved. No part of this book may be reproduced in any form without the permission of the publishers.

Library of Congress Catalog Card No. 79-54363
ISBN 0-525-03935-X
Printed and bound in Canada

"The only difference between a good carpenter and a bad one is that the good one knows how to correct his mistakes." Grampa Rewa.

Dedicated to all carpenters and to those
who are trying to become self-sufficient with
low-technology consumption.

PICTURE CREDITS

Photographs and artwork by J. Hodgkinson
Photo series, pages 96 to 104, by Fiona McCall

CONTENTS

Why Build Your Own? 9

PART 1 — GETTING STARTED

1. Choosing and Preparing the Wood 13
2. Tools You Will Need 20
3. Nails and Clamps 27
4. Joining Narrow Planks 30
5. Fitting the Pegs 36
6. The Finishing Touches 40
   Glossary of Terms 44

PART 2 — BUILDING PLANS

7. The Half-Hour Stool 50
8. Indian Chair 55
9. Sofa Sleeping Platform 60
10. Easy Bench 64
11. Pegged Desk 70

12. Quick-and-Easy Kitchen Table 79
13. Full-Wall Bookcase 84
14. Classic Coffee Table 90
15. Tab-and-Slot Bench 105
16. Two-From-One Bench and Chair 111
17. Take-Apart Storage Chest 117
18. Captain's Chair 123
19. Adjustable Sofa and Matching Chairs 132
20. Traditional Pedestal Dining Table 141
21. More Useful Plans and Ideas 150

WHY BUILD YOUR OWN?

Have you ever wanted to make your own furniture? Try it. It costs little and is creative and satisfying. The designs in this book are simple to put together, attractive, and durable. In many cases, building time is only two hours. It will take another two hours to sand and finish the wood, after which you will have a finished piece, your own creation, to use and admire. All the designs in this book can be made by using only simple hand tools.

Included are more than twenty plans for making practical things that everyone needs. They are arranged in order of simplicity, but you can really start anywhere. My designs have both the apartment dweller and house dweller in mind. I have lived in apartments for many years, so am well aware of their space and storage limitations. Apartment dwellers will appreciate the multiple functions and take-apart characteristics of most of the designs. For example, the bench-coffee table combination on page 90 is ideal for stacking magazines and newspapers, but can also be a comfortable place for friends to sit. The take-apart storage chest (page 117) is also handy for extra seating. The writing table (page 155) folds down from the wall, and is thus conveniently out of the way for most of the time.

Cost depends mostly on you and your needs. Many of the pieces can be built for less than $10.00. You can go to a lumberyard and buy an old pine plank for $2.00 that would make a great table or bench, or, you can buy select-grade pine and spend $12.00 for the same size plank. A sheet of ¾-inch good-one-side common plywood costs about $15.00, while a mahogany high-grade plywood costs $40.00. I usually use common grades of wood. Sometimes I have to work around bad knots, plane some edges by hand, but the end result is sound and usable.

Building simple furniture is satisfying and creative, as well as a lot of fun. Buy or borrow the basic tools, study the drawings and instructions, and get started.

PART 1

Getting Started

CHAPTER 1

CHOOSING AND PREPARING THE WOOD

New Wood

Most people who build furniture use new wood because it is the fastest and easiest way to get going. I recommend pine for the beginner. It is easy to work with and attractive to look at. There are many different species to chose from. I usually use white pine. Fir, spruce, and cedar are also good.

The hardwoods — birch, maple, oak, cherry, and walnut are more difficult to work with, harder to get, and are more expensive. The cost of hardwood is two to three times that of pine. Sometimes at small country sawmills where they sell rough-sawn planks one can get oak and maple for less than pine. And, if you have the time, shopping around is fun.

As a general rule, the softwoods are lighter in color with a less obvious grain. There are exceptions. For example, maple is lighter and with a less obvious grain than fir.

Judging the Wood

New wood is classed as select, common, and construction. The cheapest is construction, next common. I use common or construction grades for my furniture. Sometimes, however, it has too many knots, or it may be too crooked to join together. Only then do I buy a better grade. Even though the grades are supposed to be standardized, you will find differences and you will have to examine each piece of wood before you buy it. This is not easy to do at lumberyards — at most places you pay for your wood before you see it. I have exasperated many a lumberyard attendant by insisting that I see the wood first, but the quality of the wood in my furniture is more important to me than the impatient glare of the salesman.

First of all, some terminology: a board is a piece of wood 1 inch or less in thickness. A plank is more than 1 inch but less than 2 inches thick, while a piece of wood more than 2 inches thick is considered a timber or a post, depending on its use. Plywood, plateboard, aspenite, and all the veneers come in sheets from ⅛ to 1 inch thick.

Warping

Wood warps. That is, it becomes twisted out of shape. Warps come in many forms. One can be a bow, with the board curling up at the end so that it rocks like a rocking chair, another can twist like a corkscrew so that it will not lie flat. Or, it can cup across its width, leaving a valley along its length. A warp can also crook and wind — undulating back and forth along its length.

Some warping can be expected on most of the common and construction-grade planks or boards. It is up to you to decide what is suitable for your purposes.

The first variable is length. For example, a 16-foot board may have a bow with a "belly" 4 inches off the floor, yet when cut into 24-inch sections, will have no discernable bow. As a 16-foot board, the wood is useless, but as eight 2-foot boards, it is just fine. A twisted board is the hardest of all to work with. Always reject twisted wood as there is just no way to make it lie flat.

Cupping is also bad, as the board will split before it can be pulled flat with bolts or screws. Crooking and winding are much like bowing. If you can cut the board to diminish the warp, that's fine. Otherwise, reject it.

If there are no obvious warps, the wood is O.K. But always look first. A simple check is to lay all the planks side by side. If they lie relatively close together, they are all right. Even if you will actually not be joining planks, you will need relatively straight wood. To get an idea of how straight your piece is, sight along one edge with one eye closed. A bit of a sag is normal, but more than a bit is too much.

Shrinking and Drying

Your wood will shrink and dry after you buy it. It may have been cut months earlier, but it has probably been outside or in a damp, unheated shed. If you are joining pieces side by side, as in a tabletop, you will have to leave your boards inside where it is warm and dry for at least two weeks. Cut the wood into lengths that will slide under your bed, or somewhere where it will not be in the way. It should lie flat while drying, so that it will not warp.

Even if you are using planks that do not have to be joined, you should still bring the pieces inside for several days to dry the wood before you begin building.

Old Wood

Old wood has merits that cannot be found in new wood. Old pine, especially, is beautiful when smoothed down and finished. There will be old nail holes, minor splits, knots and, above all, a deep amber color that takes about 30 years to acquire. If you want your work to look antique, old wood with a new finish will look authentic. The best way to finish old wood is with paste wax.

If you are going to use old wood, it will involve a lot more work than new. By old wood I mean old, unpainted, rough-sawn planks or boards. I do not use old painted wood for my furniture — mainly because I do not enjoy scraping paint. It is time consuming and tedious, although the results are beautiful.

Use the same techniques to check for warps as outlined for new wood. Old wood is more brittle and will split more easily. Check for splits near the ends and around knots. If the splits are bad, that section may have to be discarded.

Smoothing

A wood plane is the main tool used for smoothing rough-sawn planks. Basically there are two types of planes:

I use the simpler model, called a spokeshave. A small one costs about $2.00. It is ideal for narrow planks and adequate, but not too handy, for wider ones.

The other type of plane, a block or jack plane, is more versatile, but costs $6.00 and up. A good one can even cost as much as $10.00.

When smoothing rough-sawn planks, never attempt to plane a wet piece of wood. The wood must be dry if you are to get a smooth surface. Wet wood shreds and splinters. Even if your plank is only marginally damp, let it dry thoroughly before working with it.

To begin planing, set the blade of the plane very shallow. That is, let it

15

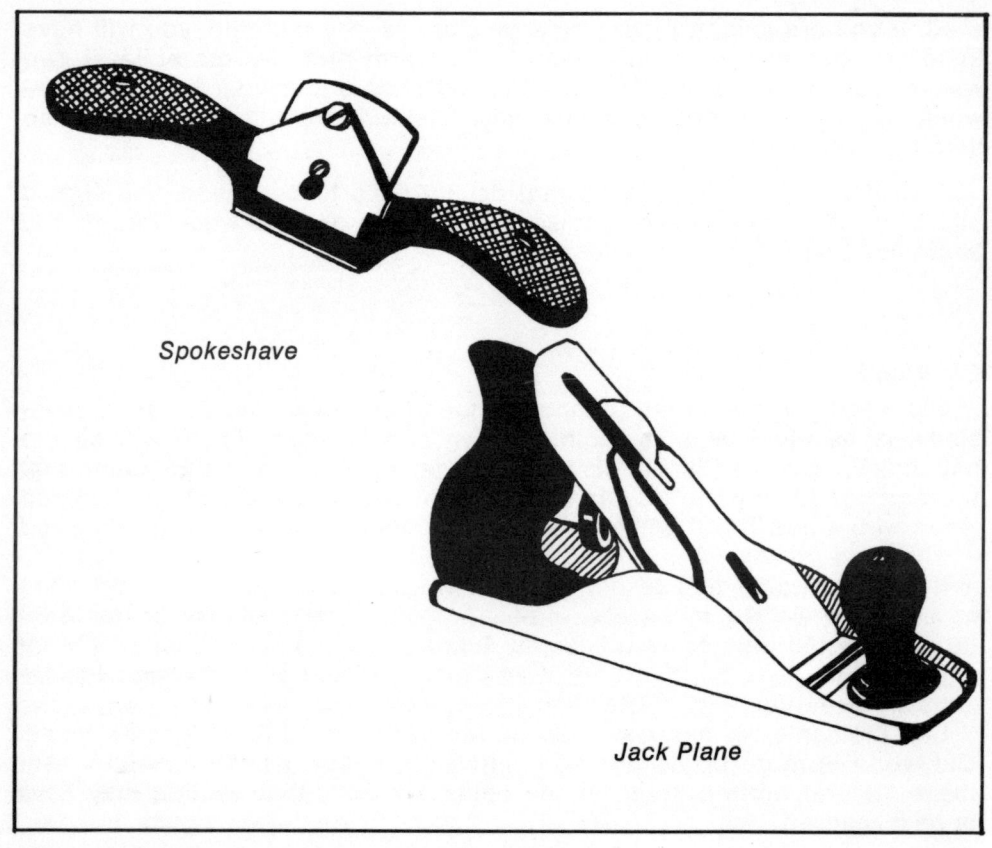

Spokeshave

Jack Plane

stick out through the carrier about 1/32 of an inch. Pull the spokeshave along the wood towards you; push the plane away from you. If you can make smooth strokes about 8 inches long, peeling off old splinters all along the way, you have set your plane properly. If it catches and sticks on the wood or bounces along the board, you have set the blade too deep.

If the blade is barely touching the surface of the board and removing almost nothing, set it a bit deeper. You should be able to slide the plane along the board smoothly to get a smooth finish. If you work with short jerky motions, you will have a rough finish. Always push (or pull) your plane with the grain, that is, along the length of the board. Try to work evenly along the whole plank, or you may make low spots.

Plane all four sides of the plank to a moderately smooth finish. You will do the remaining smoothing with coarse sandpaper (40 or 60 grit), but do this after you have completed your piece. If you do all your sanding now, you will probably be duplicating some of your effort later.

Sharpening Your Plane

If the plane gets dull, that is, when it will not peel off a thin layer of wood, it will have to be sharpened. Take it out of the carrier, noting how to put the plane back together as you disassemble it. Use a whetstone or other knife-sharpening tool. Old wood has years of dirt and grime ground into it, so by the time you finish planing the second plank, you may have to sharpen your plane.

Cement

The worst dulling material on wood is cement. Do not try to plane a board that has cement on it — unless you are really desperate.

Repairing Old Wood

Sometimes you will get a very attractive old plank with lots of character, but with a split in it. You can repair many of these splits. However, if the split is down the center of the plank, forget it.

To fix a split, you need a wood drill, doweling, and some glue. For example, I once had an old plank that I wanted to use for a bench top. There was a split along the side, about 3 inches in from the edge. I knew that I had to cut some slots out, which made matters worse. Here is how I corrected it.

Drill through the edge of the split piece, drilling 1 to 2 inches beyond the split. The longer the better, but the dowel will hold with as little as 1 inch of doweling in the main piece. I use ⅜-inch doweling, hence a ⅜-inch

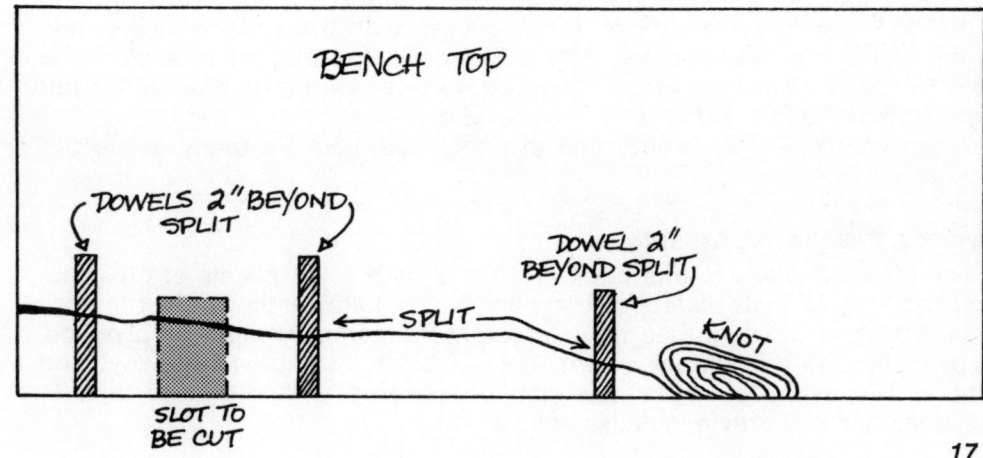

Top of Easy Bench showing repaired split. Note the split and the dowels repairing it on either side of the tab.

---

drill bit. Clean the shavings out of the hole and put in a few drops of glue. Cut a dowel to fit the length of the hole flush with the surface. Apply glue to the dowel and tap in place with a hammer. You may need a clamp to hold the doweled pieces (see section on clamps) as the glue dries. Do not work on that piece of wood until the glue is dry.

When your plank is smooth and in one piece, you are ready to start.

Plywood, Plateboard, Aspenite

The plywood plans in this book are for ¾-inch 4 x 8 sheets of plywood. You can use ¾-inch plateboard, aspenite, or whatever they call it in your area. Plateboard, which has approximately the same strength as plywood, is available with a variety of veneers — birch, walnut, mahogany, and others. The exposed edges can also be covered with a veneer tape to make the finished article look like solid wood.

Aspenite, another plywood substitute, is usually cheaper than plywood, but not as readily available in small towns. It comes in 4 x 8 sheets, ¼ to ¾ inches thick, with about the same strength as plywood. It is made by grinding aspen trees into chips, then gluing the chips together. Its main drawback is that its surface is not smooth, thus it is not suitable for a desk or table, but can be used for benches and shelving. Because of its coarse surface, aspenite looks better when varnished, rather than painted.

The cheapest and easiest material to acquire and use is fir plywood, which is good only on one side. This means that there will be knotholes on one side, but not on the good side. Actually, if you plan a natural finish, you may, in fact, treat the knotty side as your good side. If you are going to paint your furniture, you must use the good side as the outside surface. Apply an undercoat first, otherwise the grain will show through the paint.

If you want a natural finish with plywood, neither the spruce nor the fir grains are anything to rave about. The veneer plywood or plateboard will give you a much prettier finish. Remember though, that a spruce or fir plywood sheet costs $12.00 to $14.00, while a veneer sheet ranges from $22.00 to $25.00 and maybe more, depending on the veneer and where you live.

You can also get good-both-sides plywood, or the much cheaper construction-grade plywood with knotholes on both sides.

The patterns in this book are for good-one-side plywood, with the knotty side on the inside.

CHAPTER 2

TOOLS YOU WILL NEED

For the simpler pieces, you will need a crosscut saw, a keyhole saw, a carpenter's square, and a drill and bits. The other tools listed below are required for the more complicated pieces. However, at the beginning of each plan, the tools that are needed for that piece are listed. Here is a description of some woodworking tools and their uses.

Crosscut Saw

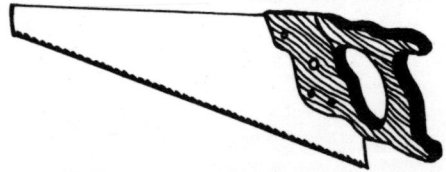

Every carpenter uses a crosscut saw more than any other tool. I recommend that you get a handsaw with a 22 to 26-inch blade and with 8 points (teeth) per inch. This is the most common type of handsaw. You can get one at any hardware store for $5.00 to $15.00. Buy a good saw, and keep it where it will not get dull or rusty. I have a good 26-inch saw that is teflon coated. This saw is used to make straight cuts in boards and plywood.

Keyhole, Compass, or Hole Saw

This is a short saw (14 to 16 inches long) with the blade tapering to a point. The blade is tapered so that a cut can be made from a hole drilled in a board. The names keyhole, compass, hole, refer to the type of blade. The handles are different on each type. These saws are used to make slots in tab-and-slot furniture or cuts between two points that do not end on the edge of the board, as between the tabs on the box design in Chapter 17. Cost: $3.00 to $8.00.

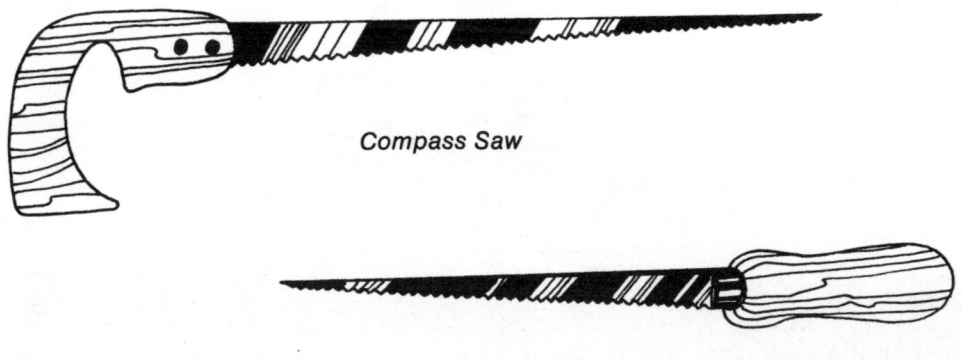

Compass Saw

Keyhole Saw

Coping Saw

The coping saw is used for cutting circles, rounding corners, and cutting out designs. The blade is hung in a removable bow-like handle. When you start a cut that is set in from the edge of a board, put the blade through a drilled hole, then attach the handle.

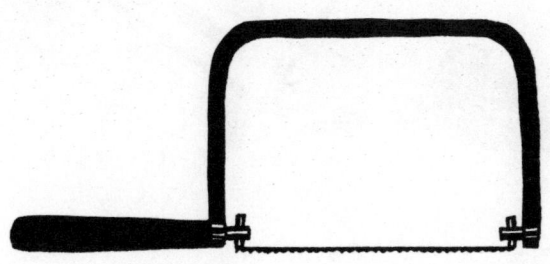

Sabre or Jig Saw

This is the second electric tool that I would buy — with an electric drill being the first. The sabre saw is handy for cutting designs, circles, tabs and slots, and rounding corners. Your local store sells them for about $15.00 for a small brand-name tool. It replaces the keyhole and coping saws. A word of warning: take it easy with light-duty electric tools. Do not try to force them to cut too fast.

Drills

After the saw, the drill is the most-used piece of equipment. I recommend buying a ¼-inch electric drill. You can get a medium-quality drill for $12.00 to $15.00 at your local discount store. The ¼-inch drill makes screw holes, 1-inch holes for pegs, and starter holes for the keyhole saw. It will also cut larger holes with an expanding bit or hole saw, if you take it easy. Forcing the drill into a plank until it stalls will ruin the drill. When and if your drill case gets too hot to hold comfortably, or starts to smoke, give it a rest.

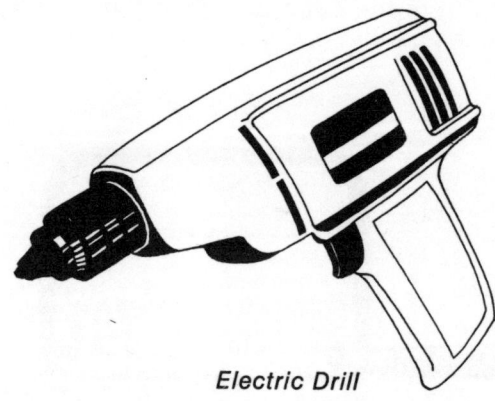

Electric Drill

Hand Drills

For drilling holes larger than ¼ inches, you will need a **Carpenter's Brace** (Cost: $7.00-$10.00).

For making holes ¼ inch or smaller, you require a **Pinion Drive** or **Egg-Beater** type small hand drill (Cost: $5.00-$8.00).

You can also make small pilot holes without a drill; to do this you will need a set of **Gimlets**.

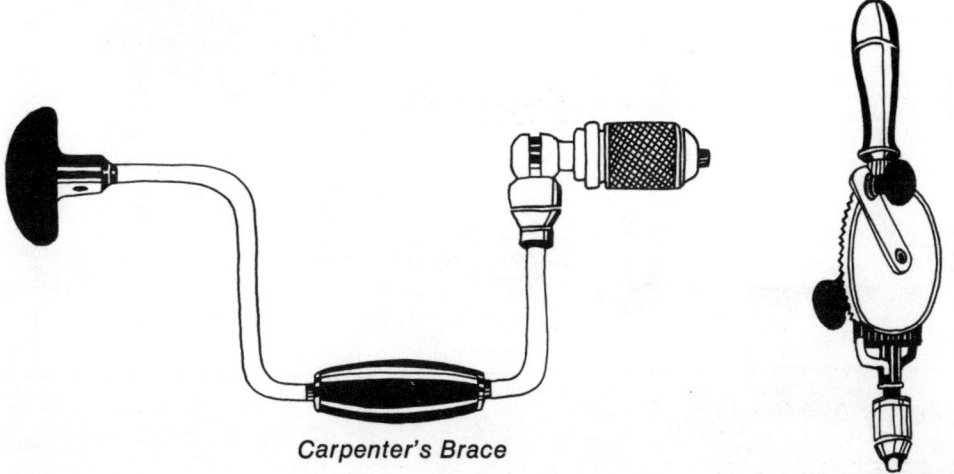

Carpenter's Brace

Pinion Drive Hand Drill

Drill Bits

The flat wood-boring bits for electric drills are much cheaper than the square-shanked bits for a carpenter's brace. A set of wood-boring bits for the electric drill costs about $2.00 to $3.00 for the ⅜ to 1-inch size. A set of small bits up to ¼ inches is about the same price.

Expanding bits or a hole saw are used for making holes from 1 to 2½ inches in diameter and cost from $2.00 to $3.00. I recommend the hole saw for making holes in plywood and 1-inch boards, but for planks and large blocks of wood you will need an expanding bit.

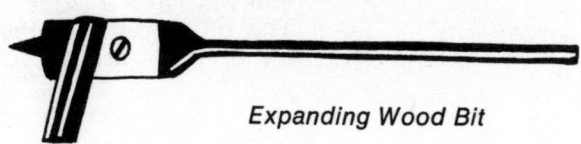

Expanding Wood Bit

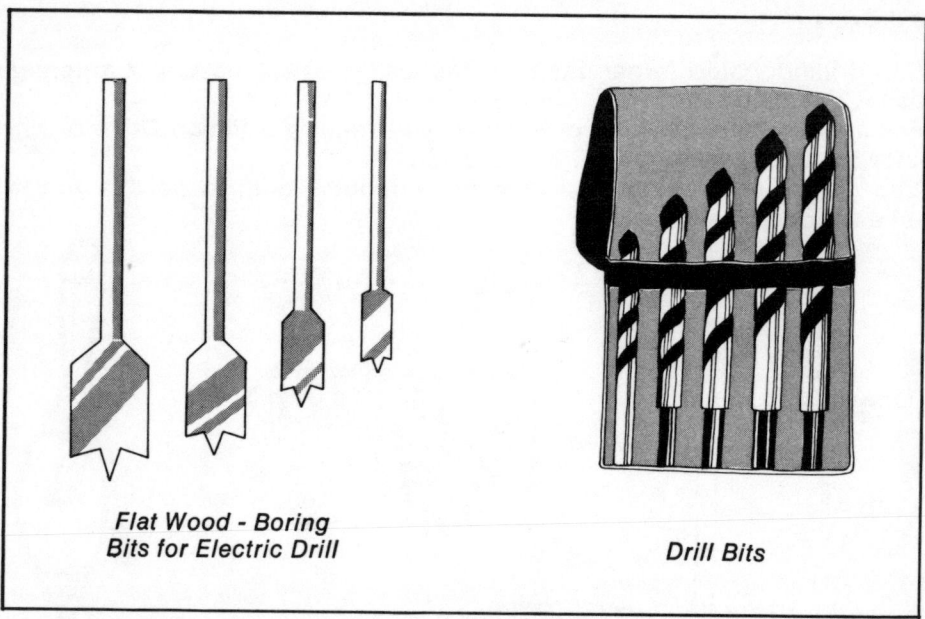

Flat Wood - Boring Bits for Electric Drill

Drill Bits

Combination Countersink Drill Bit

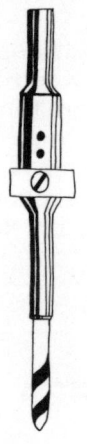

This is a handy item if you are setting a lot of flat-head wood screws. It is a combination bit — it can drill three different-sized holes with one drill bit. It drills the pilot hole, the screw-shank hole, and the countersink hole at one time, which saves changing drill bits. Combination countersink drill bits are available at larger hardware stores. They come in the same numbered sizes as screws; thus if you are setting a No. 8 screw, you will need a No. 8 combination bit. The bit adjusts for the depth of hole for different length screws.

Square

A useful and necessary tool. Get the large carpenter's square, 16 inches x 24 inches, costing between $5.00 and $8.00. This tool is necessary to ensure that cuts are straight across the boards, and that corners are square when joining two pieces of wood.

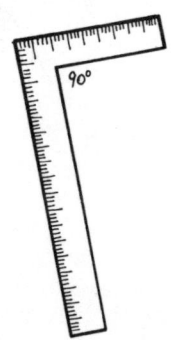

Plane and Spokeshave

These two tools are used for smoothing rough wood, straightening warped wood or uneven edges, or removing a bit of wood when something does not fit. When joining planks edgewise, or using old wood, you will need one or the other. A plane is more versatile than the spokeshave, but the plane costs between $7.00 and $15.00, while you can get a spokeshave for $2.00 to $6.00.

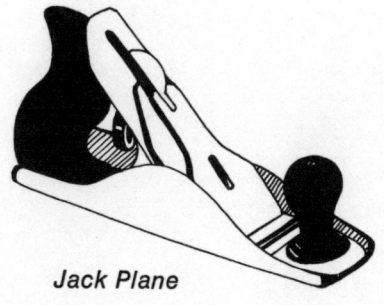
Jack Plane

Spokeshave

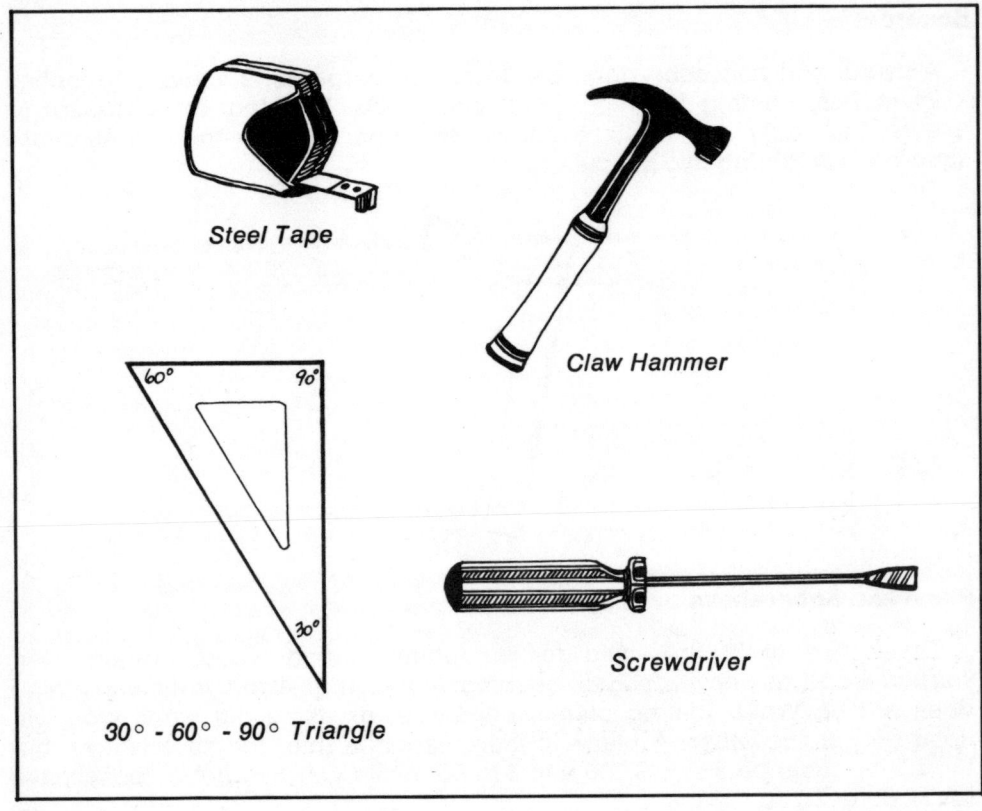

Steel Tape
A handy item. Get a 6-foot tape.

Claw Hammer
Always useful. Get a 12-ounce head.

Screwdrivers
Get the correct sizes for your woodscrews.

30°-60°-90° Triangle
Necessary for some of the designs in this book.

CHAPTER 3

NAILS AND CLAMPS

Nails and Their Uses

As a general rule, I do not use many nails, but I do specify them for backing pieces on joined planks and for making clamps. I use common wire nails for nearly everything. They have a smooth shank and a medium-sized head.

Finishing nails are headless nails used when you do not want the head to show. They can be tapped in below the surface of the wood with a larger nail or punch, and become nearly invisible.

The length of the nail is determined by what you want the nail to hold. If you are fastening a 1 x 3 to a 2 x 8, do not buy a 3-inch nail! You do not want the nail tip to come out on the other side. Remember that a 1-inch board is actually ¾ inches thick and a 2-inch plank is actually 1¾ inches thick. Thus the total thickness of the pieces you are joining is 2½ inches. In this case, a 2-inch nail would be just right. The diameter of a nail is proportionate to its length, so width is not a worry.

As a rule of thumb, to determine the length of nail to use when nailing a piece of wood to a larger piece, consider this. If you wanted to nail a 2 x 2 to a wall stud you want the nail to be into the wall stud a distance comparable to the thickness of the 2 x 2. Thus, because a 2 x 2 is actually 1¾ x 1¾, a 3½-inch nail would do. For example, one use for a finishing nail is to nail a strip along the edge of the desk on page 70. For this you would have ⅜-inch thick molding and, because the desk would probably be bumped a lot, I would use a 1¼-inch finishing nail.

Twist shank nails hold a bit better than the smooth-shanked wire nails. They come as finishing or construction nails, but do not use a twist shank nail where you might want to pull it out later.

Clamps Used for Gluing or Doweling Planks Together.

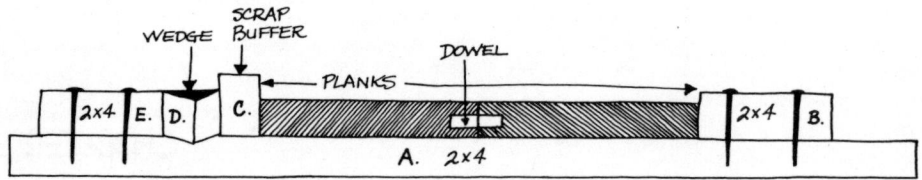

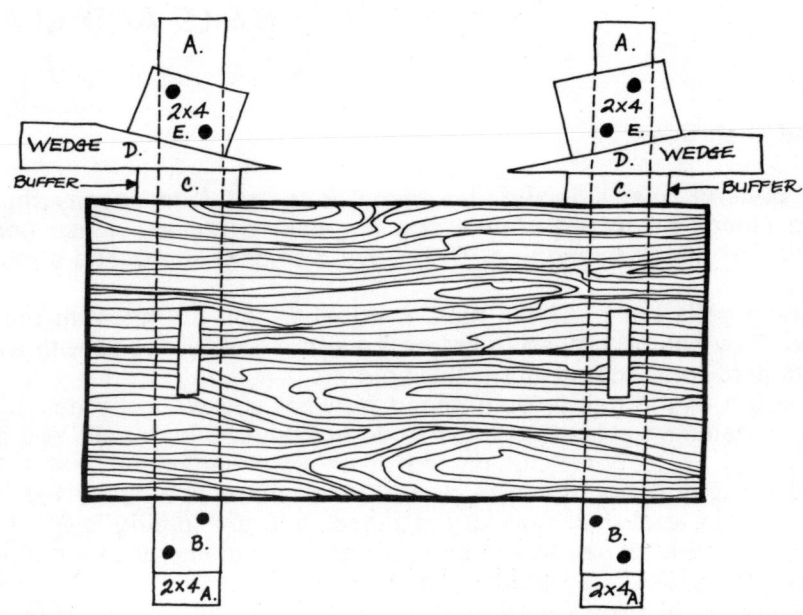

1. The longer 2 x 4 piece should be about 18" longer than the total width of the planks to be joined (A).
2. Nail a 2 x 4 near the end (B) as at right.
3. Put the planks against that.
4. Add buffer block (C).
5. Add wedge (D).
6. Nail another 2 x 4 (E) next to the wedge, roughly at the same angle as the wedge.

Clamps

For gluing and doweling planks together, clamps are needed to hold the planks together while the glue is drying. You can buy some pipe clamps at the hardware store for about $10.00 each. You will need two of these. Or, you can make wooden clamps yourself which also work quite well.

Find a 2 x 4 or piece approximately that size that is about 18 inches longer than the width of the two planks you are joining. Nail a piece of 2 x 4, about 4 to 6 inches long, at one end. Lay the planks you are going to join on the 2 x 4 and put a scrap of 1-inch wood that is 2 inches or more wide next to the planks, but lying on its edge. Make a wedge out of the 2 x 4 and lay it beside the 1-inch piece, but do not have its maximum width over the long 2 x 4. Take another 6-inch long piece of 2 x 4 and slide it next to the wedge and at roughly the same angle as your wedge. Nail this 2 x 4 piece to the long one. (See diagrams opposite.)

Make up two of these clamps before gluing the planks. When you are using them, clamp one near each end of the plank that is being glued. You can get by with just two clamps by gluing one plank and letting it dry befor gluing another.

CHAPTER 4

JOINING NARROW PLANKS

You may have to join planks when you want to make, for example, a 14-inch wide bench, but can get only 12-inch (11¼-inches) wide planks at the lumberyard. Here are two methods that I use to join planks when faced with this problem.

Get planks which are about half as wide as the desired width (the plans in this book are flexible as to width). Leave them in a room with approximately the same temperature and humidity as the room where the furniture will eventually be. It is necessary to let the boards shrink and dry. Even wood that has been cut for several months will still shrink considerably.

Leave the planks in a warm, dry place for at least two weeks. When dry, try to match the edges. Some boards will fit together better along one edge than another. Flip them over, end-for-end, or in any other combination until they lie beside each other with the least unevenness. Also, remember that the shorter the board, the shorter the warp, and thus less crack. So, cut your planks to length before joining. If they still do not come together, get your hand plane out and smooth down the high spots. Mark the board with a pencil where the planks touch, then plane down that spot until it no longer prevents the boards from coming together. You may have to do this several times, but only plane a little off at a time, or you may make low spots out of formerly high spots. Do it slowly, eye the edges, and you will eventually get it right.

When the planks fit together suitably, you can join them. I say suitably, because small cracks the thickness of a matchbook cover or so will be filled with glue or varnish and are of little consequence.

Method One — Backing Pieces

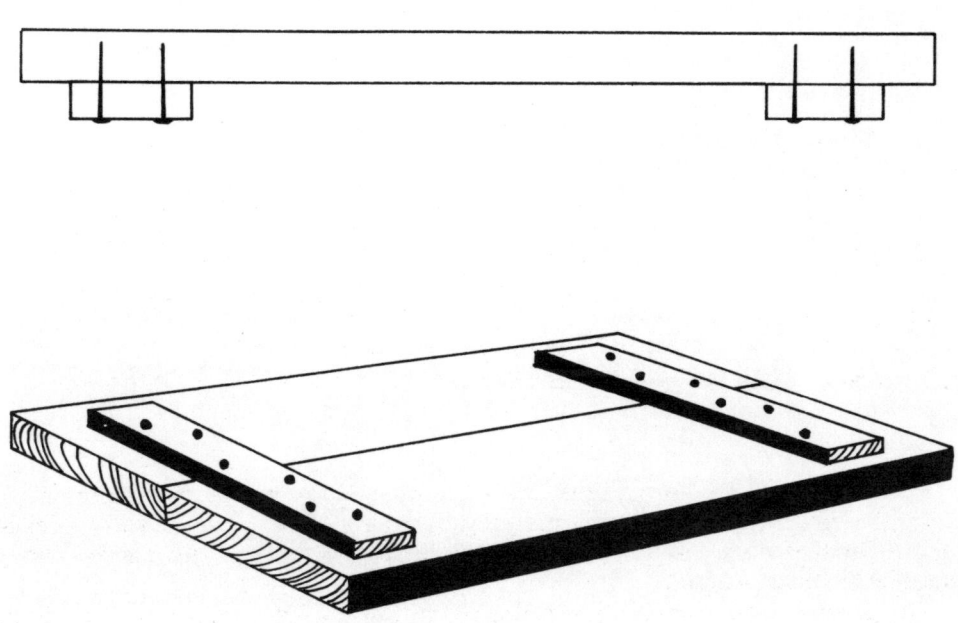

The easiest way to join your planks is with backing pieces. The advantage of this method is that it is fast and easy. The disadvantage is that in the temperate zones we have a considerable variation in the weather. Remember that closet door that in the spring and early summer hardly closes when it is damp; yet in the winter when the furnace makes the house really dry, it rattles in its frame? That is what will happen to your planks. They will shrink in the winter and expand in the damp weather. Boards joined in this manner may separate, then join together again.

If they separate too much, do not join together again, and you are bothered by it, here is what you do: Simply take the backing pieces off and push the planks closer together. Or, you can just watch the passing seasons and comment on what happens. Do not worry too much about it, as there will be no great gaping holes. If your planks are dry to begin with, they will only open enough to just see through, and will not spoil the look of the piece.

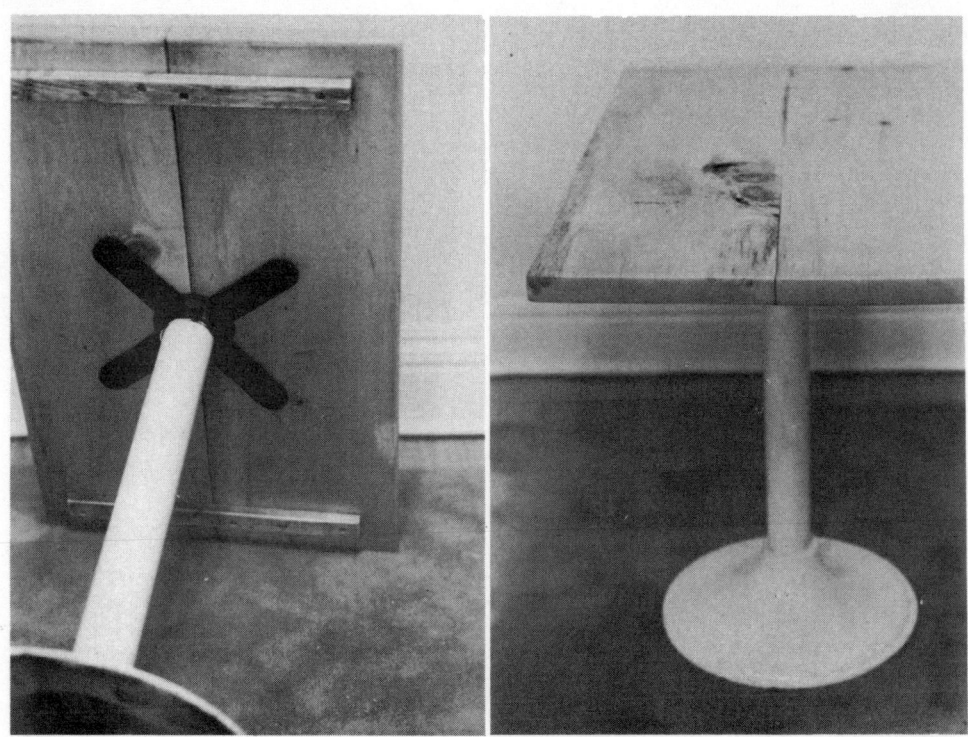

Plank tabletop showing backing pieces as in Method One, and planks joined.

For backing pieces, take some 1-inch boards about 2 to 3 inches wide and cut them to about 4 inches smaller than the width of the planks that you are joining. Attach them about 2 inches from the end of these planks. Put some ordinary white glue on the backing pieces and nail or screw them in place. Make sure that your planks are held together tightly when you attach the backing pieces. Use screws or nails that will reach about three-quarters of the way through the main piece of wood. Use one nail or screw near each edge of each piece joined, on each end. Do not put all the nails or screws in a straight line, as that may split your backing piece.

You should put the backing pieces at or near the end of the planks because this will prevent the ends from separating and raising one edge higher than the other. This is apt to happen when boards shrink and stretch.

If one plank is slightly thicker than the other, plane down the higher edge after the glue dries.

Method Two — Glue and Dowel

A more professional, but more difficult and time-consuming way of joining planks, is to glue and dowel the edges. This is the best method as, if the wood shrinks, cracks will not open at the joint. Planks joined together in this manner act as one plank, shrinking and stretching across the whole width, as there are no backing pieces to hold them apart. You will need clamps for this method. Consult section on clamps, page 27.

You will need some dowel stock (¼-inch or ⅜-inch) and some wood glue. One 3-foot length of doweling will be more than enough for any piece of furniture.

Lay the planks together as described above, with the edges fitting close together and with no gaps showing. When they are lying side by side, ends flush, cut them to length, the way you want the boards to look when finished. Mark the places for the dowels with a pencil.

Measure about 2 inches in from the end of the plank and make a pencil mark across the joint between the two planks, marking on both of the planks. Do this about every foot along the plank, ending with a mark about 2 inches from the other end. These are the places where the dowels will join the planks. Now, tip the boards up on their outer edge, with the ends even, just as they were before. With the planks on edge, mark across the edges at the pencil marks, using your square.

The marks must be accurate, or the planks will not fit together. Use the edge of a book, a piece of wood, or anything that is about half the thickness of the plank as a guide (about ⅞ of an inch for a 1¾-inch plank). Hold it flush with the outer edge (top surface if the boards were lying flat) and mark the middle of the edge of your plank at these marks across the thickness of the plank. You **must** be accurate and consistent in this marking to make the joining procedure work.

The point at which the lines intersect is the place to drill your hole for the dowel. Use a wood bit the same size as the doweling. Try to drill the holes as straight as possible in from the edge. Drill the holes about 1½ to 2 inches deep, but make them all the same depth. Dab a bit of paint on your drill shank, or mark it with a file so you know when you have gone deep enough. Cut your dowel pieces so they are just shorter than twice the depth of the holes in each plank. Clean the shavings out of the dowel holes before proceeding.

You can buy insets which will aid in marking the dowel holes. They are available at your hardware store. With these, you mark and drill the dowel holes in one plank, insert the insets for that side dowel into those holes, then push the boards together. The inset will make a mark on the other plank where the matching hole should be drilled.

You will need clamps soon, so get them ready now. (See section on clamps, Chapter 3.)

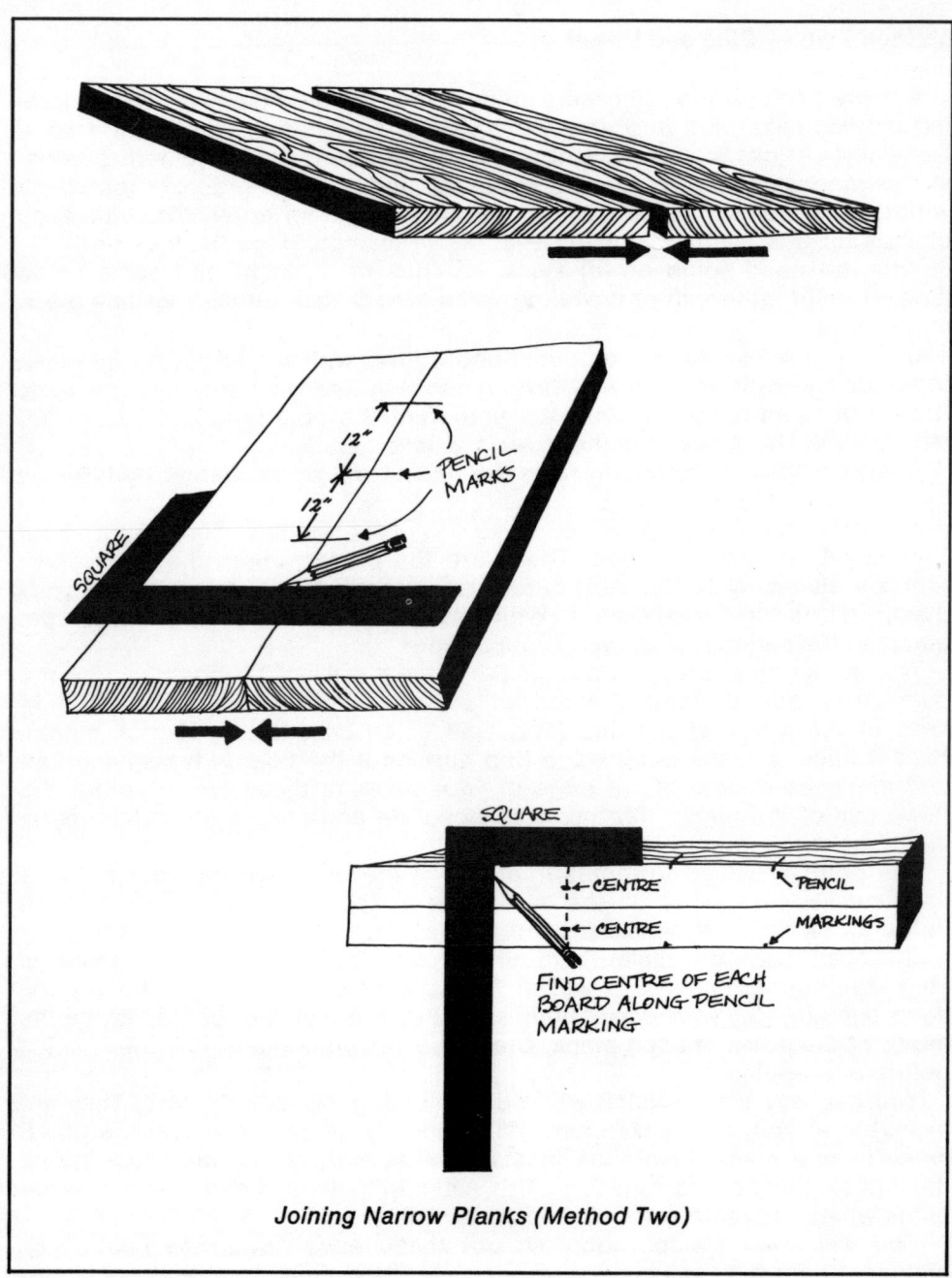

Joining Narrow Planks (Method Two)

When you have all the dowels, holes, and planks ready, put a few drops of wood glue in each of the dowel holes and smear a dab of glue on the dowel itself. Then, partially insert the dowels into the holes on the edge of one plank. Lay a zig-zag bead of glue along the edge of one plank. Make sure that the planks are free from sawdust, dirt, or grease. Insert dowels part way into the holes on the edge of the opposite plank, inserting them all at the same time. Tap the two planks together with a piece of wood and a hammer (hit the piece of wood which lies against the plank, thus protecting the plank from the hammer).

When your pieces have been glued together, wipe off the excess glue and put the planks in the clamps. The planks must lie flat in the clamps. If one plank is higher than the other on the top surface, that is not serious. Plane the higher edge down, after the glue has dried.

If your planks do not go together, you have:
a) made your dowels too long, or,
b) drilled the holes for the dowels crooked and they do not match.

If this happens to you, you must
a) shorten the dowels
b) redrill the holes, or,
c) use joining Method One.

After your planks have been joined and the glue is dry, you are ready to begin making your own furniture.

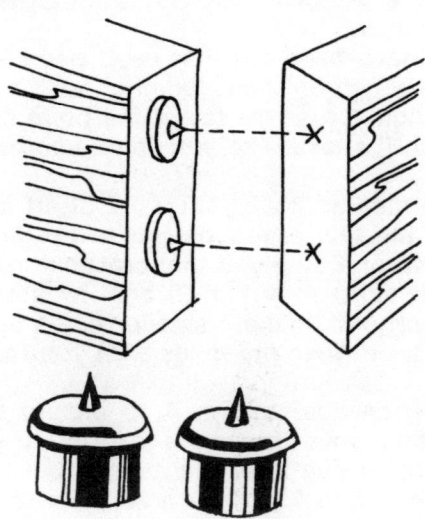

Insets for Doweling

CHAPTER 5

FITTING THE PEGS

Several of the furniture designs in this book use the tab-slot-peg principle, whereby pegs have to be fitted to each individual tab-and-slot. The process is described here, as it is essentially the same for all of the pieces that use this method of fastening.

To begin with, do not attempt, especially at first, to make the slot exactly the same size as the tab. Allow at least ¼ inch extra for the slot. Even ½ inch extra is not unsightly.

When all the pieces have been cut that need pegs fitted, put the whole thing, whether table or bench or chair, together, and have a friend hold it. Make a mark with a pencil across the tab at the point where it is flush with the plank through which it sticks. The pieces of wood **must** be held tightly together. (Fig. 1.)

After all the tabs are marked, take your work of art apart. Make a crosshatch at the center of the tab, perpendicular to the first mark. Now, take your 1-inch wood bit and drill a hole at that crosshatch, but the drill should overlap on the first line (Line A in Fig. 2) only by about ¼ of an inch. If you do not have a 1-inch drill, make 4 smaller holes in a 1-inch square as shown in Fig. 3. Cut out between the holes with your coping saw, keyhole, or sabre saw. (Fig. 3.)

The hole has to overlap across Line A to ensure that the pieces will tighten against each other when the peg is inserted. If you do not have the overlap, you may have your peg tight in the hole, but the pressure will not force the boards together. See Fig. 4 for a solution to this problem.

When all the holes are cut, reassemble the whole piece of furniture. Now, take that little scrap of wood that you cut off to make the tab, and split it with a knife or hatchet into approximately a 1-inch square, leaving it the same length, about 3 to 4 inches. (Fig. 5.)

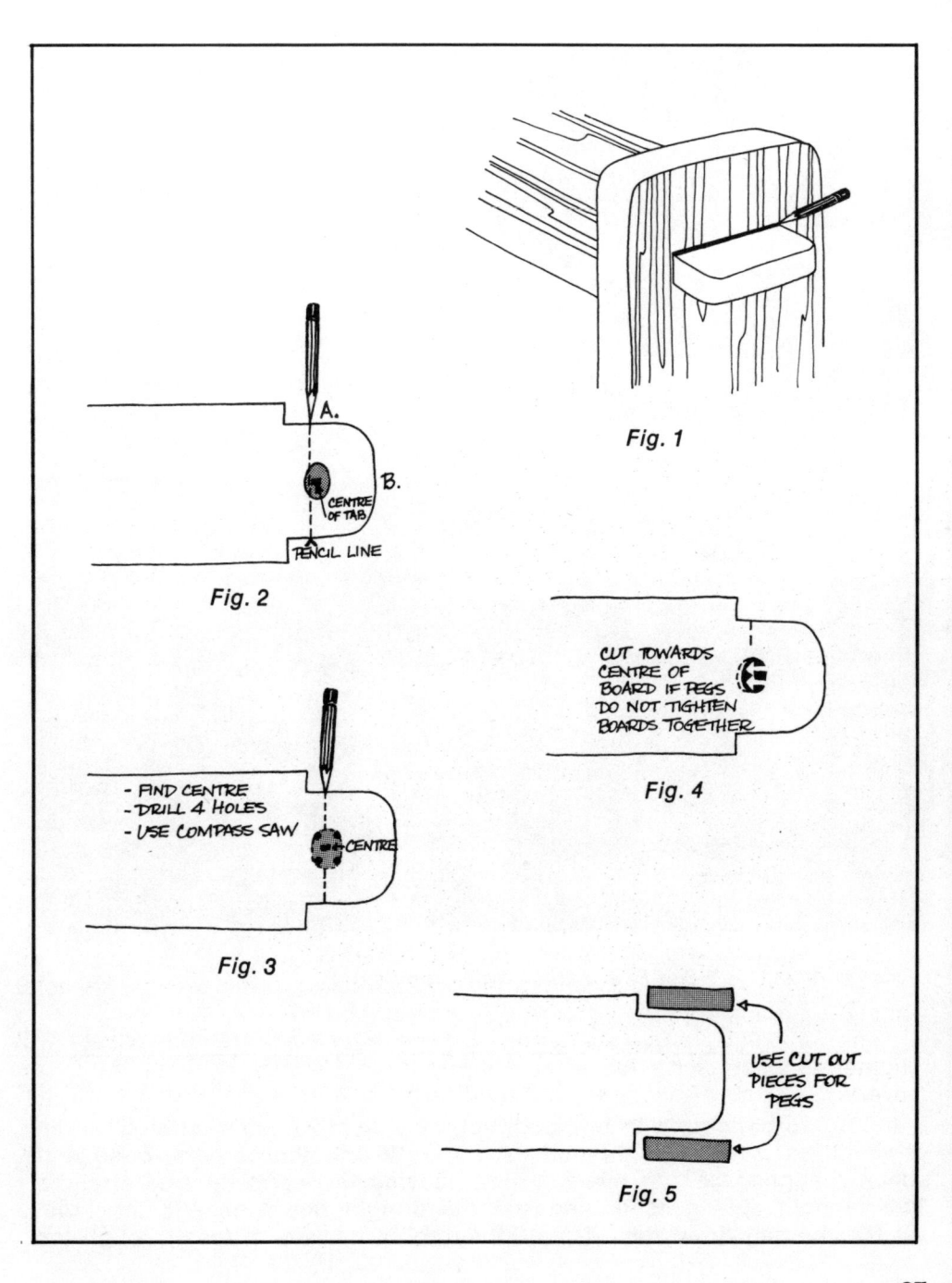

Fig. 1

Fig. 2

A.
B.
CENTRE OF TAB
PENCIL LINE

Fig. 3

- FIND CENTRE
- DRILL 4 HOLES
- USE COMPASS SAW

CENTRE

Fig. 4

CUT TOWARDS CENTRE OF BOARD IF PEGS DO NOT TIGHTEN BOARDS TOGETHER

Fig. 5

USE CUT OUT PIECES FOR PEGS

Close-up of the Tab-Slot-Peg method of fastening.

If you are building with plywood, you may want to use a different scrap of wood, as plywood is difficult to shape. Whittle the corners round and shape a slight taper on one flat side, leaving the opposite side straight. This straight side goes flat against the upright board next to the hole. Whittle the peg down until it fits tightly about halfway or less through the

38

hole. I say halfway or less, as the wood may shrink or your peg may squash a little, so you need some extra tightening length. Do not hammer the pegs really tight. You risk splitting the tab or the peg if you do. I push mine in with my thumb, then give it a light rap with the hammer. The pegs have to be snug to keep tables or chairs from wobbling, but any tighter than snug will not increase their strength.

If you find that the pegs are all tight in the holes, yet the boards are not tight against each other, you have to change your peg holes a bit. Enlarge the holes towards the center of the board, that is, away from the end. (Fig. 4.)

After all the pegs have been fitted, number them with a pencil on the side that goes against the plank. Also, mark the inside of the hole with a corresponding number. The pegs must always be returned to their original place, as they are not necessarily interchangeable.

Smooth and sand your pegs, especially on the ends, to expose the cross grain. If your piece is to have a natural finish, finish the whole thing the same way. If you plan to paint it, you can leave the pegs unfinished to give the piece variety. I did this with the storage chest described on page 117 and the results were very attractive.

CHAPTER 6

THE FINISHING TOUCHES

Veneer Taping

Veneer taping is a thin strip of wood used to cover the edges of plywood and plateboard.

The process is used to give a finished look to plywood or plateboard that has been veneered with a better-quality wood. By gluing veneer taping to all exposed edges, the finished piece has the appearance of solid mahogany, birch, or whatever veneer you are using. Contact cement is used to glue the veneer taping to the wood.

The taping comes in 8-foot long pieces, either in straight strips or in rolls. Usually it is 1 inch wide. When applying it to ¾-inch plywood or plateboard, first glue the taping on full width. After the contact cement has dried, trim it with a sharp knife or razor blade.

Always use contact cement, as it eliminates the need to hold the taping to the edges until the glue dries. Contact cement fixes the taping to the surface immediately. Have the taping cut to the proper length, and well lined-up before having it touch the edge.

There is a knack to trimming the taping without splitting it: when you cut it in one direction, it will split out towards the edge of the taping. This is the right direction to cut. Sometimes a split will run over the edge of your plywood. To prevent it from getting worse, start cutting in the other direction. The right cutting direction depends on the grain of the veneer. Thus, on a long strip of taping change your cutting direction several times.

Whatever you do, do it carefully and slowly. You will get it right if you take your time to puzzle it out.

The Finish

After your piece of furniture has been completely assembled, it has to be finished. This entails sanding it smooth, exposing the grain, and then painting or varnishing it.

When sanding, use a padded sanding block. I use a 2 x 2 scrap of wood with an old sock rolled over it (three layers thick). My block is about 4½ inches long. I tear a sheet of sandpaper in half, wrap it around the block and sock, and then rub it back and forth in short, easy strokes. A word of warning — never sand wet wood, as the sandpaper shreds and gouges it, making the wood even rougher.

Before sanding, have an assortment of sandpaper ready, from very coarse grit (No. 60) to very fine (No. 200). You will need the coarse grit to smooth the edges and corners and to expose the cross section of grain at the ends of the boards. The place where the saw cut the board ends is usually the roughest area. Take your heaviest grit paper and work on these parts first, rubbing across the width of the board or across the thickness. It does not matter much which way you sand here, as the grain does not run straight in either direction.

When the grain comes up, the end of the board will be fairly smooth. Now is the time to change to a medium-grit paper to finish the job. Coarse paper leaves marks which resemble scratches; the finer paper removes these scratches.

To sand the rest of the area, use a medium-grit paper. Sand with the grain, that is, along the length of the board. Never sand across the width of the boards, as that leaves many bad scratches. It will be rougher around the knots, so spend a little extra time on them. Sanding also makes the knots look more attractive.

When the whole area feels smooth to the touch, take some fine paper and give it one last quick going-over. Fine-sanding removes fine splinters and scratches left by the coarser grit papers.

Now wipe the wood clean of any particles of wood or dust before applying varnish or paint.

Use any clean soft rag — cotton, flannel, or knit. Old shorts, socks, underwear are ideal. After wiping the wood clean with the rag, rub your hands over the whole area. Sometimes you may get splinters, but it adds an extra something to the wood. Your hands will wipe off sawdust that the cloth left behind. Also, it gives the wood a color and quality which you can get in no other way. There is something about perspiration which adds to the look of wood. Also, rubbing is a very pleasant sensation! Your wood now looks and feels smooth and clean, it smells good, and your hands have detected rough spots that need a little extra attention.

For a paint or varnish finish, you will need a brush. The brush must be clean and dry, and free from dust and dirt. If it is not, you will get a rough finish. If the brush is an old one, clean it thoroughly, as it may be saturated with old paint, varnish, or solvent which could discolor your wood or varnish.

Varnishing

I use a urethane, satin (non-gloss) varnish on most of my furniture. It gives a clear, hard, and waterproof finish that is also very attractive.

First, put on a generous first coat, literally soaking the wood. With the brush work it into the grain and all knots.

After the first coat dries (read the directions on the can), your piece may feel rough in spots. There may have been some sawdust or other foreign matter on the varnish. Now is the time to remove it. Sand with fine paper, and pick off any foreign matter with your fingernail. Afterwards, sand these areas lightly with fine sandpaper. When you are satisfied with the smoothness of the whole area, and have wiped the sawdust off, apply one or two more coats of urethane.

The room where you varnish your furniture should be free of dust, as dust particles will get on your wet varnish. Not realizing this, many people sweep their workshop floor just after they have varnished something. Naturally, all that dust and dirt sticks to the tacky varnish, leaving a porcupine-like finish.

If, after your last coat of varnish is dry, the surface is still rough in spots, **lightly** sand the rough spots with some extra fine sandpaper. This final sanding will take off the sharp points, but will not harm the finish. Remember to sand in the direction of the grain.

Painting

If you are going to paint your furniture, use the same sanding procedure as outlined above. The first coat of paint is an undercoat. When the undercoat dries, check for smoothness and foreign matter. Correct imperfections by lightly sanding with fine paper, wipe the surface clean, and then apply your finish coat. Having an undercoat will give you a much better finish than if you only apply a top coat. Wood without an undercoat will show the grain through the paint. The grain looks good with a varnish finish, but it is ugly through paint. This is especially true if you want a glossy finish with bright colors.

Paste Wax

Sometimes people who like a natural finish on their wood get tired of seeing varnish shining back at them, and they switch to paste wax. Also, for furniture made with old wood, a paste-wax finish is prettier and suits the wood better. Old pine, particularly, really likes a paste-wax finish. The wax soaks in well and lasts a long time. However, if you paste-wax a surface that gets lots of use, such as a table, you will have to re-wax frequently.

Any standard book on furniture-making will tell you about exotic waxes from the tropics, in addition to the two most common, paraffin and beeswax. All these waxes are usable, available from any building supply store, and need not be passed up. However, if, like me, you want a functional finish with a minimum of fuss, go to the local store and buy a good, common name-brand furniture paste wax right off the shelf, take it home, and apply it. Here is the right procedure:

1. Sand and smooth wood as for painting and varnishing.
2. Wipe off all sawdust and dirt.
3. Put a good dab of wax on a soft cloth (old T-shirts or sweatshirts are great for this) and rub it into the wood using a circular motion.
4. After evenly covering the wood with a light coat, let the wax set for several hours. Then buff lightly with a dry cloth.
5. Apply further coats of wax (another two or three) in the same manner until you are satisfied with the finish.

GLOSSARY OF TERMS

Here are some definitions of the most commonly used woodworking terms. Become familiar with them and you will find the designs and directions in Part Two very easy to understand.

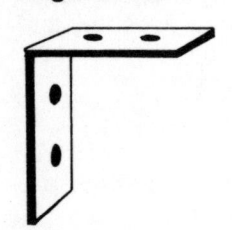

Angle Brace Used under shelving and any 90° joint between two pieces of wood where the attachment must be hidden from view. Also helps to support and reinforce corners. Available in various sizes from ¾ inch per side and up.

Aspenite This is a plywood substitute, sold in sheets like plywood. Basically, it is aspen trees ground to chips, then glued together. It does not have a smooth surface, but is useful for shelving or benches. Aspenite is of comparable strength to plywood, but is usually cheaper.

Board Any piece of wood 1 inch or less in thickness.

Carriage Bolt Round-headed bolt with a square shank at the head. Used for joining two pieces of wood where a smooth head is desired. See Diagram D, page 47.

Countersink A shallow hole drilled into a piece of wood to allow a bolt or screw head to fit flush with, or lower than, the surface of the wood.

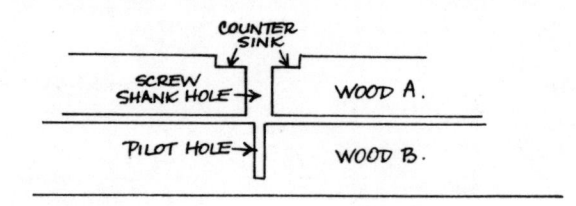

Combination Countersink Drill Bit See Drill Bits in Chapter 2.

Dowel Round shaft of wood. Dowels are available in sizes from ¼ to 2 inches in diameter and in varying lengths from 3 to 16 feet.

Flush A term used to indicate that two edges or pieces of wood are exactly even.

Glides Round metal discs found on the ends of sofa legs, resembling large tacks with polished heads. They are handy for raising a solid-legged table or desk high enough off the floor to prevent wobbling. To install, drill a pilot hole, then tack in place.

Glue I use only two types of glue. For general-purpose gluing, doweling, joining planks, and backing pieces, I use ordinary white wood glue. For gluing on veneer taping, I use contact cement, as it immediately holds the piece in place.

Hole Saw There are two different types of hole saws. One, also called a compass saw or keyhole saw, is used to start a cut from a drilled hole. It is a scaled-down hand saw, with similar teeth and a pointed end.

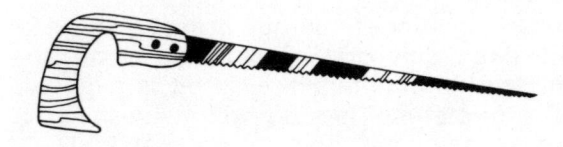

Hole Saw (cont'd) The other type of hole saw is used with a drill and will cut a circular hole in a board. It will cut holes from ¾ to 2½ inches in diameter. Select the size you want by removing the other cutters.

Lag Screws A stout wood screw with a bolt head on it. Always use a flat washer under the head. See diagram opposite.

Nails See section on nails, Chapter 3.

Pilot Hole The starting hole for a screw. It is the first hole to be drilled when setting a screw. The sequence is: Drill the pilot hole with a drill slightly smaller than the diameter of the threads on the screw. Drill the pilot hole at least as deep as the screw is long. Next, make the countersink hole. I usually use my ⅜-inch wood-boring bit and cut a hole about ⅓ of an inch deep for a flat-headed screw. Next, with a drill the diameter of the screw shank, drill through the pilot hole, **but only the depth of the top piece of wood—not through the whole depth of the pilot hole.**

If you are attaching hinges, corner braces, or metal strapping, you need only drill a pilot hole to set the screw. A combination countersink drill bit is available at larger hardware stores. This tool will make the pilot hole, the screw-shank hole, and the countersink hole all at once. See drill bits in the tools section Chapter 2. See illustration for Countersink, page 44.

Plank   A piece of wood more than 1 inch thick.

Plateboard   Also called composite board, pressboard, or particle board. It is similar to plywood, but is a mixture of sawdust, chips, and other materials, saturated with glue and pressed into sheets to resemble plywood. It usually has a wood veneer over it. Plateboard can be used in place of plywood for practically everything.

Plywood   Several thin layers of wood laminated together. The usual sheet size is 4 x 8. Also available in larger sizes.

Screws for Wood   **Flat-headed wood screw:** the most commonly used screw for making furniture. It holds well and the head is easily countersunk to fit flush with the surface.
Round-headed wood screw: has a high rounded head which stays above the surface of the wood. Used when a heavier-duty screw is called for, especially when using hardwoods. Will take more strain without splitting the wood. Round-headed screws are also commonly used when attaching a piece of metal to wood when the head is not countersunk. All screws are sold by a number indicating their diameter. The smaller the number, the thinner the screw. I usually use No. 6 to No. 10 screws.

A. Wood Screw (Flat Head)

B. Round Head Screw

C. Carriage Bolt

D. Lag Screw

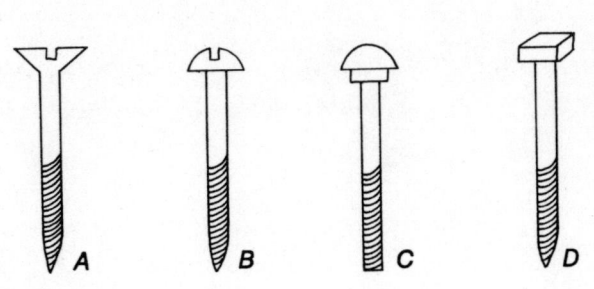

Screw-Shank Hole　See Pilot Hole

Square　A term meaning that a corner, a piece of wood, or a cut is at a 90° angle to another edge, cut, or piece of wood. Also refers to the tool — the carpenter's square.

Veneer　A thin layer of wood that has been peeled off a log and laminated to other woods. Also a thin layer of expensive, good wood such as walnut, birch, maple, or mahogany. Usually an overlay on plywood or plateboard.

Veneer Tape　A thin strip of wood, usually 1-inch wide and 1/16 inch or less thick which is glued on the edges of plywood or plateboard to make it seem solid walnut, birch, or any good-quality wood. See Veneer Taping, Chapter 6.

PART 2
Building Plans

50

CHAPTER 7

THE HALF-HOUR STOOL

This handy fold-away stool can be built in about half an hour. It is ideal for apartment dwellers who occasionally need extra seating, but do not have space for spare chairs. These stools can also be used for the patio, for camping, or for your fold-away writing table. (Page 155.)

Children like them if scaled down to their size, but they usually pinch their fingers a few times before figuring out how to handle them.

	YOU WILL NEED
Wood	one 1" x 3" 12' fir, spruce, or pine board cut into the following lengths:
	four 22" long
	two 17" long
	one 15¼" long
Cloth	one piece 15" x 36" canvas, leather, plastic, upholstery material or any strong cloth
Hardware	two ¼" x 2" carriage bolts
	four ¼" flat washers
	four nuts for the carriage bolts
	twelve 1½" No. 6 flat-head wood screws
	two dozen ½" carpet tacks
	wood glue
Tools	saw, square, drill and bits, screwdriver, hammer

Building Instructions

Cut the 1 x 3 to the above lengths. Round the ends of the 22-inch lengths as shown in Fig. 1. I have found that a coffee mug is ideal for marking the rounded ends and a one-quart paint can is about right for marking the half-rounded ends. Cut all four pieces the same. (Fig. 1.)

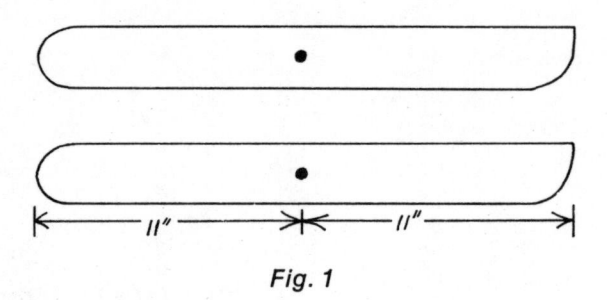

Fig. 1

Drill a ¼-inch hole in the exact center of all four pieces. Match the pieces into two pairs. Each pair should have the half-rounded ends facing each other as shown in Fig. 2. Slip a bolt through the first board, insert a flat washer between the boards, put the bolt through the second board, then add a flat washer and a nut. Tighten this nut snugly. Then screw another nut on. Tighten these two nuts on to one another so that they jam and do not loosen.

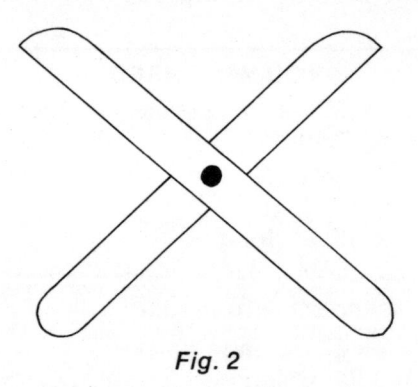

Fig. 2

Set the two pairs of legs parallel to each other, with the rounded heads of the bolts on the outside. Lay the one 17-inch piece across the legs. It will be flush with the top of the half-rounded end, but against the flat side of the board — not the rounded side. The rounded sides should be flush with the outermost edge of both pairs of legs. Check to see that the pieces are square; drill pilot holes for your screws, then the shank holes. Apply some glue and attach the board with two screws at each end. (Fig. 3.)

Tip the boards over so that they are on their other side. Attach the other 17-inch piece to the outside legs, but about 1 inch below the level of the bolts. This piece should be flush with the outer edges, and square with the legs. Attach it with glue and two screws at each end. (Fig. 4.)

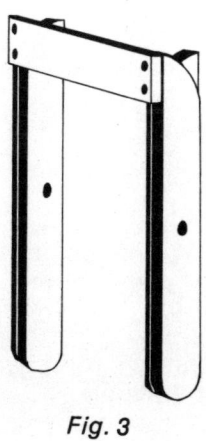

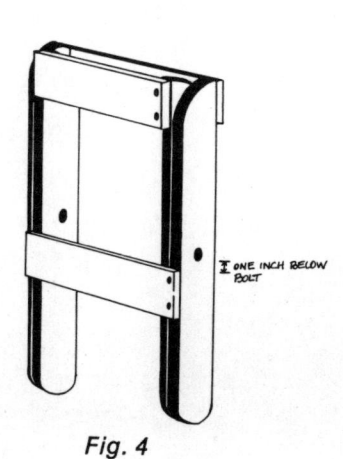

Fig. 3   *Fig. 4*

The last piece goes across the top of the inner legs. It should be flush on the ends and the top edge. Attach it with glue and two screws at each end.

You now have the completed frame. Put a finish on it now, before you attach the cloth, to avoid getting paint or varnish on the material.

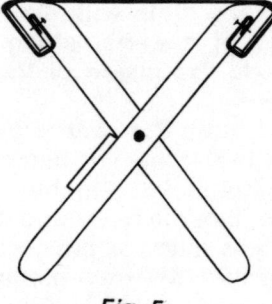

Fig. 5

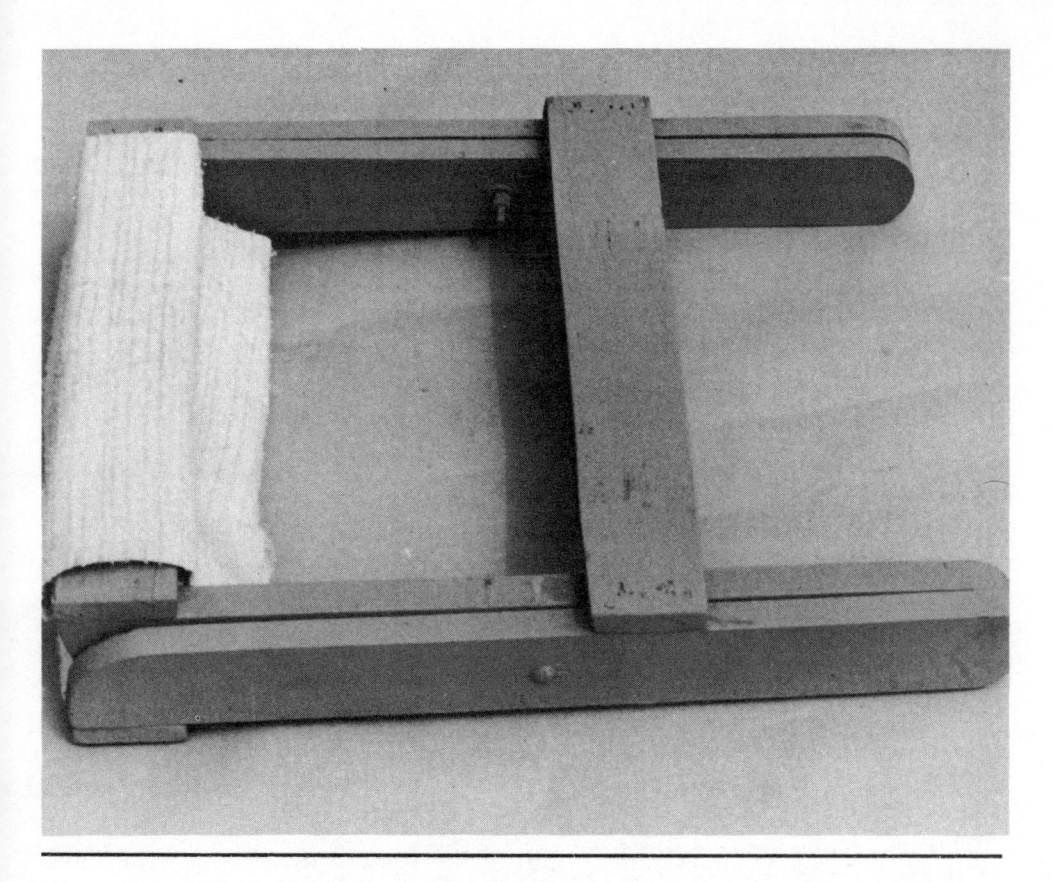

The Half-Hour Stool closed and lying flat.

If you are using cloth that will fray, fold it under along the edges and sew along this seam. Attach the cloth with ½-inch carpet tacks. Begin by folding under about 1 inch of material along the width, and tack this double layer of material on to the inside of the 17-inch piece, using one tack an inch.

When one end is attached, wrap the cloth around the 17-inch piece, over its top edge, and across to the 15¼-inch piece. The stool should expand to a total outside width of about 16½ inches. While someone holds the stool in that position, wrap the cloth around and up under the 15-inch piece, fold the rest under, and mark or pin it. Lay the stool flat and tack the cloth on to the inside of the 15¼-inch piece, using one ½-inch carpet tack every inch. (Fig. 5.)

CHAPTER 8

INDIAN CHAIR

This chair is one of the first pieces that I built. It is patterned after a chair that Indians use in the mountains of Mexico. Surprisingly comfortable, even with no padding, it is one of my favorites and can easily be built in less than two hours. The wood will cost between $5.00 and $8.00. Construction-grade lumber will do. I have made a 12 and a 14-inch wide chair. A wider plank can be cut to similar proportions.

YOU WILL NEED	
Wood	one 2" x 12" 8' pine, cedar, or fir plank
Tools	saw, steel tape, carpenter's square, keyhole saw, drill and bits

Building Instructions

Square the ends of the plank, then cut it in half. Cut one of the 48-inch long pieces as shown in Fig. 1. The square part will be the seat of the chair. Cut 3 inches off each edge of the plank, starting 12 inches from one end (Fig. 1). On the 12-inch square end, cut both end corners off diagonally as shown in Fig. 1, measuring back 2 inches on the side and 3 inches across the front. Cut at this diagonal line.

The Indian Chair complete.

The Indian Chair parts.

The other 48-inch piece has to have a hole cut through it to slide the seat part through. Measure 12 inches from one end and mark a line across the plank. Then measure 3 inches in from both edges of the plank, marking on that line. Check to be sure that the remaining space between the two 3-inch marks is equal to, or greater than, the narrow part of the seat plank. Now, measure the thickness of the seat plank and make your hole about ⅛ of an inch bigger than that. Mark out this rectangle above the line 12 inches from the end of the plank. Drill a ¼-inch hole in each corner to start your keyhole saw, then cut, making the hole. (Fig. 2.)

Try to have the hole the same size as the thickness of the other plank. If the hole is too large, your chair may lean back too far. However, this can be corrected by inserting a wedge. Cut the bottom end of the upright piece (with the center hole) off at a 60° angle. (Fig. 3.) While not absolutely necessary, the wedge will add to the stability of the chair, making it less likely to tip forward.

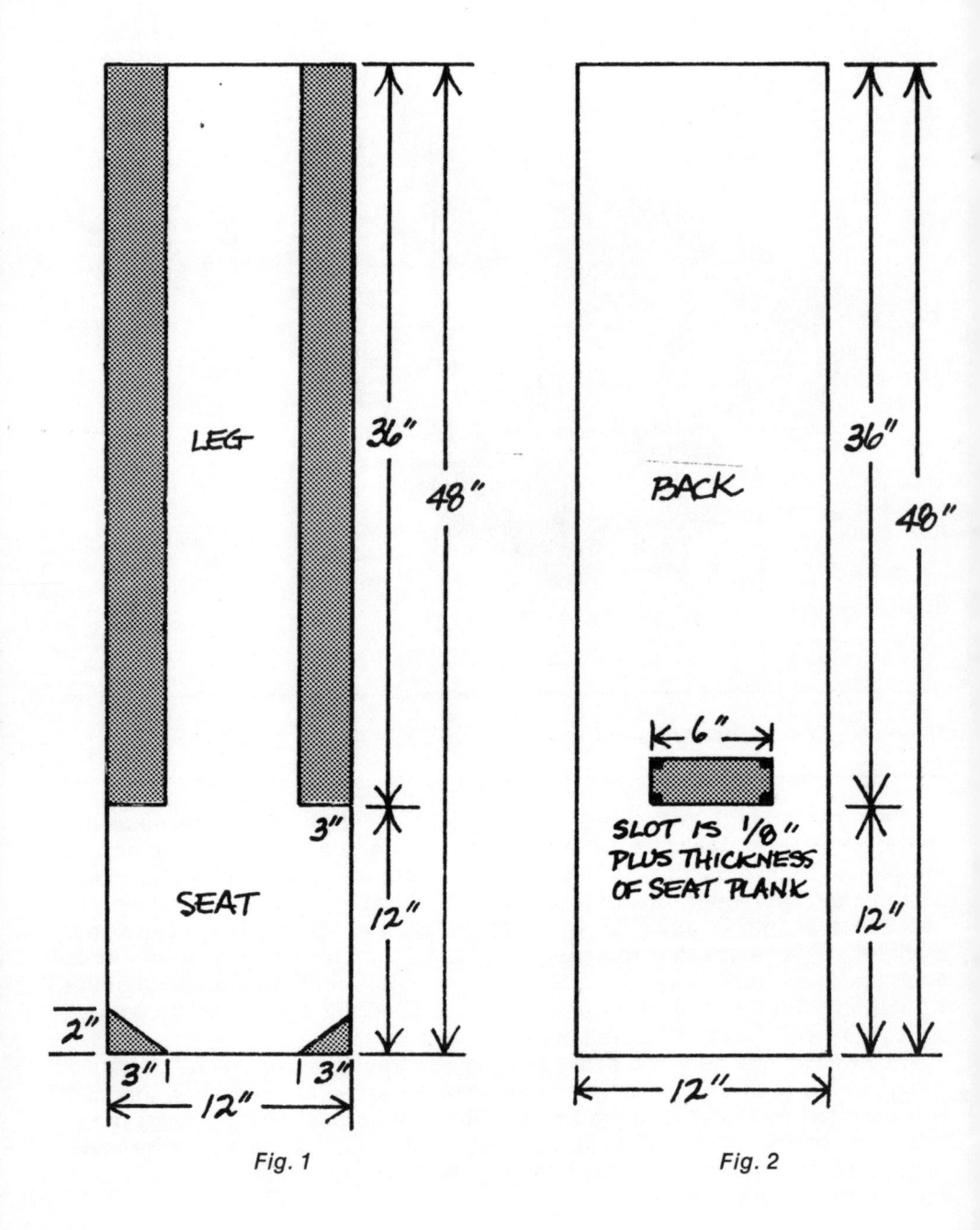

Fig. 1

Fig. 2

Fig. 3

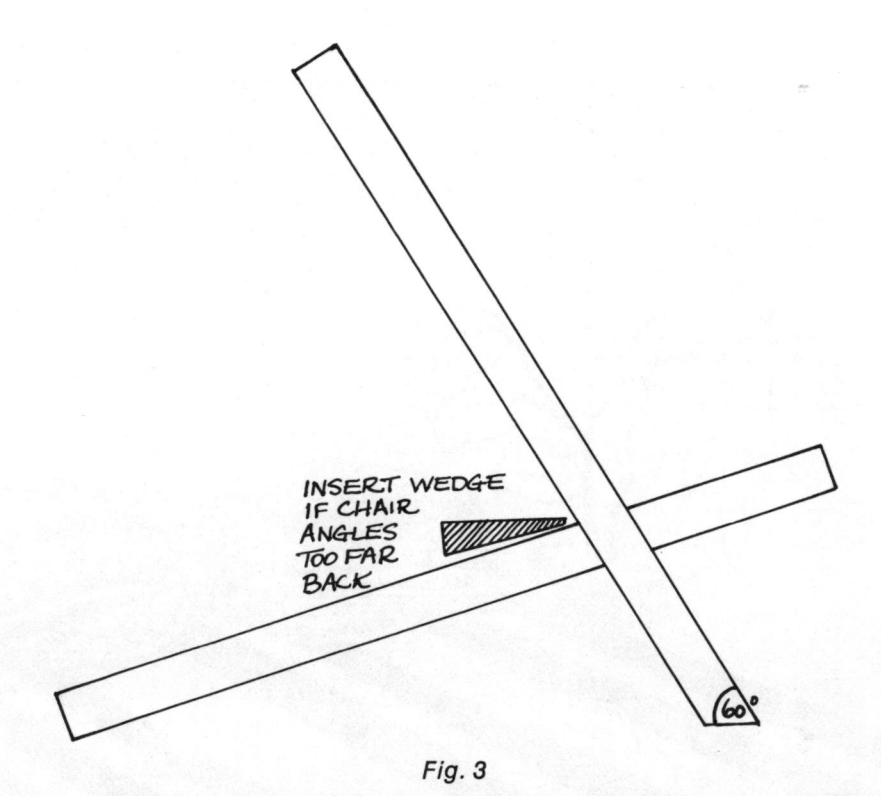

Now slide the seat plank through the slot, and you have a great chair. You can add a pad for the seat if you like, but I find this design comfortable without any padding.

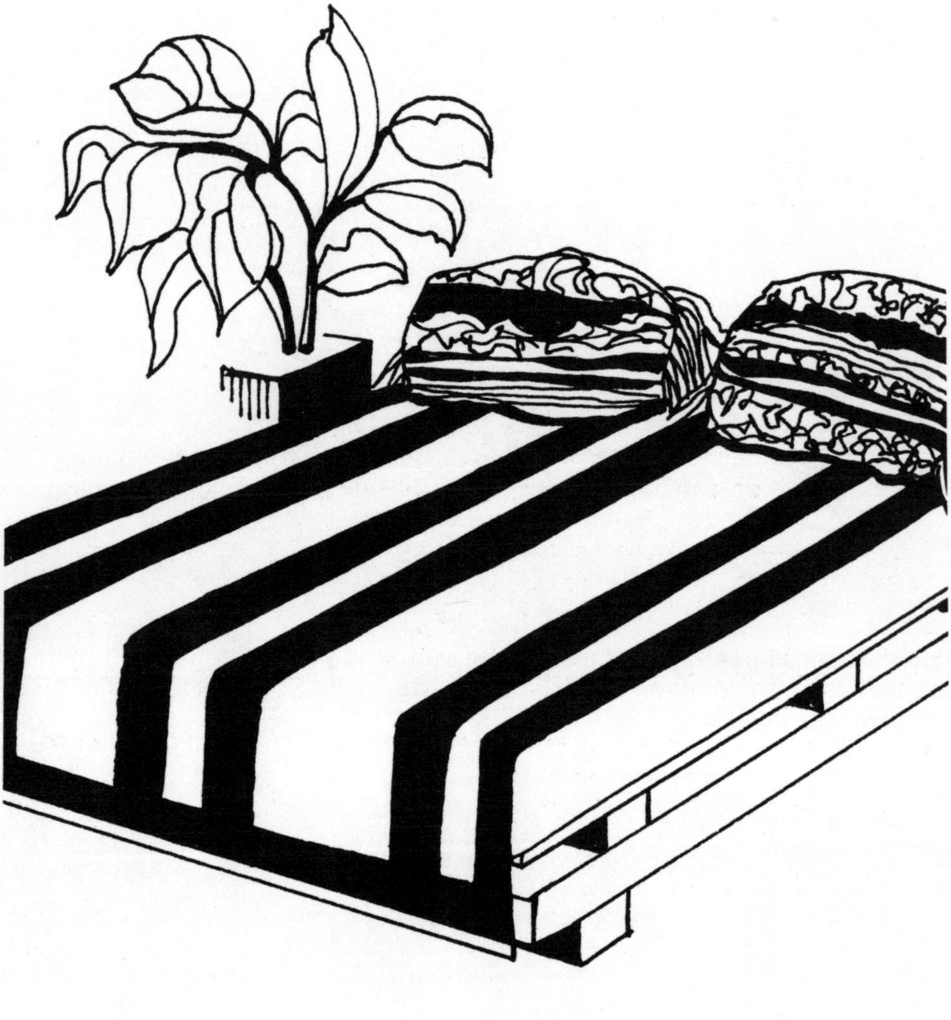

CHAPTER 9

SOFA SLEEPING PLATFORM

Here is an attractive, dual-purpose design, suitable both for sleeping or lounging — so practical where living and sleeping space are one and the same.

First decide what size you want. Thirty inches is the minimum width for a single sleeper. A double mattress is 54" wide, and the most common length is 6 feet.

	YOU WILL NEED
Wood	4" x 4" cedar fence posts or other suitable wood
	ten ½" dowels 6" long
	one sheet of ½" plywood, plateboard, or aspenite the size of your mattress
Hardware	six nails 1¼" long
Tools	crosscut saw, square, drill and ½" bit, hammer, tape measure

Building Instructions

Use 4 x 4 fence posts (usually cedar), available at any lumberyard. They are cheaper than regular-timber 4 x 4s.

To make the frame, you will need five 4 x 4s the width of your mattress and two 4 x 4s the length of your mattress, plus one piece of ½-inch plywood the size of your mattress. You will also need ten pieces of ½-inch doweling 6 inches long.

Lay out the 4x4s as shown in Fig. 1, with two short pieces on the floor and the two longer pieces lying across the edges of the shorter pieces. Use a carpenter's square to ensure that the structure is reasonably square.

Take your drill bit and drill a hole through the long 4 x 4 and into the shorter one, until the hole is 6 inches or more deep — but not necessarily through the shorter 4 x 4s. Try to hold all the pieces as straight as you can during this operation.

After you have drilled the hole in one corner, pound in one of the dowels. Keep moving around the structure until you have all the corners drilled and doweled.

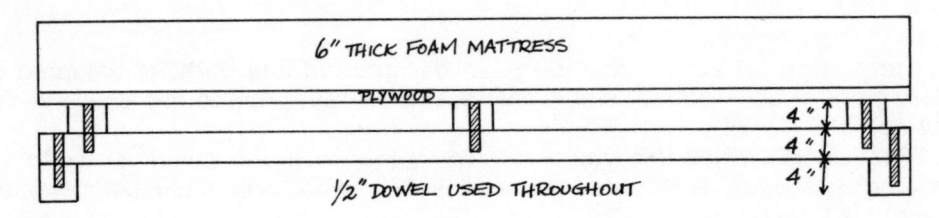

Fig. 1

Take the remaining three 4 x 4s and lay them on the long pieces. The end 4 x 4s must not be directly over the previous two shorter 4 x 4s. If they were you would have problems dismantling the structure (Fig. 1). Therefore, place them just inside far enough from the ends so that you can still pound out the lower dowel. Center the third short piece on the long pieces between the ends. If you do not keep everything square, or if the dowels are drilled in crooked, your frame will not sit flat after it is squared for the plywood top. Now drill holes and insert dowels the same as for the first set of dowels.

When the frame is complete, lay the sheet of plywood on the frame and nail it into place with a few nails on each 4 x 4. Do not put too many nails in because, if you ever have to take it apart, the more nails, the more difficult it will be. The sleeping platform or sofa is now ready for a mattress. Cover it with a favorite blanket or spread.

If you use foam, it should be at least 6 inches thick. If you use an old cotton or kapok mattress, a few inches of foam below it will make it much more comfortable.

To dismantle the structure, remove the plywood and simply pound the 4 x 4s apart. Number all the pieces so that you can assemble it again easily.

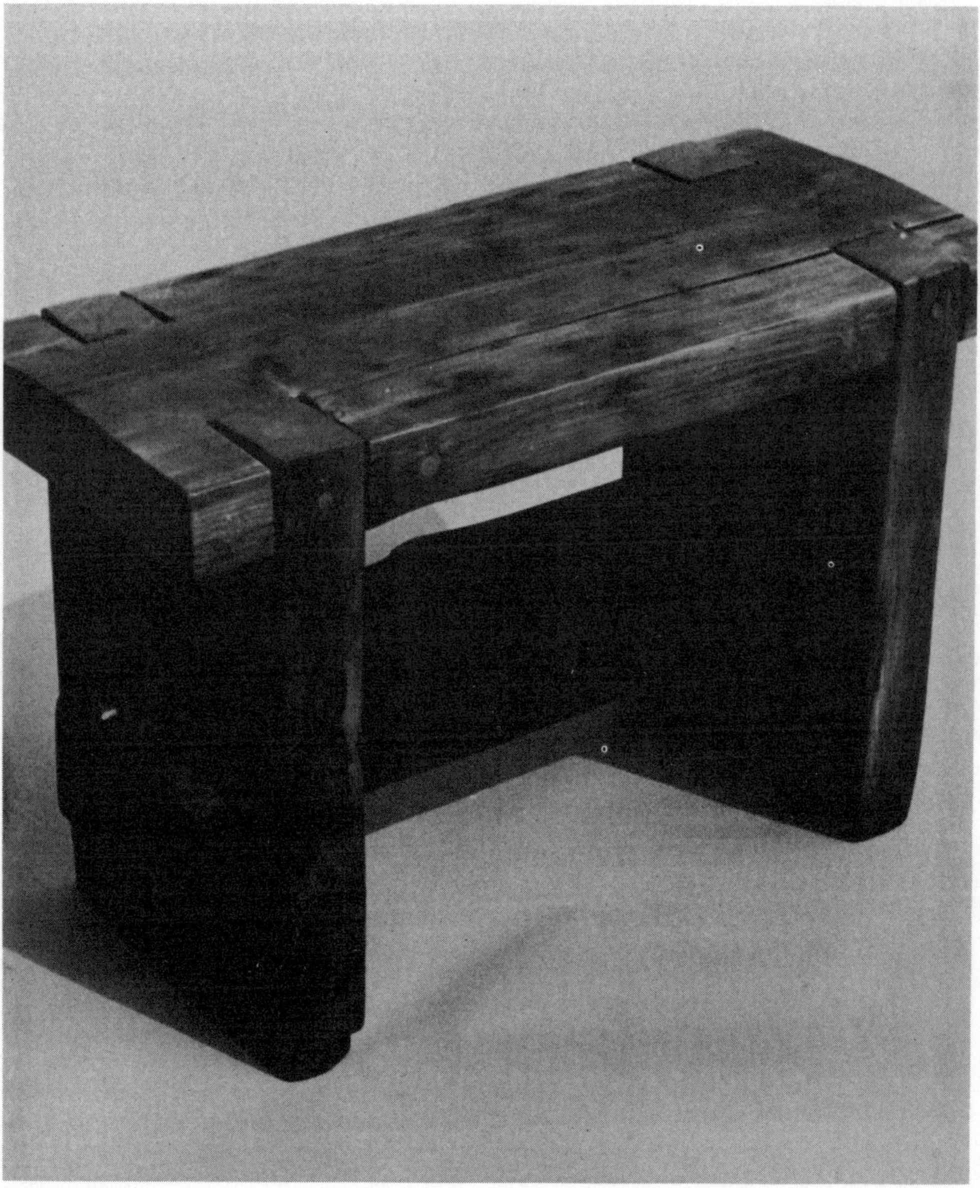

CHAPTER 10

EASY BENCH

This little bench is easy to make and very useful. It differs from the coffee table on page 90 in that there are no angled cuts. I use it as a footstool, a bench, or a coffee table. Mine is 24 inches long, 10½ inches wide and 15 inches high. I made it from an old spruce plank that used to be part of the coal bin in the back shed.

Decide how long and how wide you want your bench. A 10-inch width is about minimum, with 12 inches being ideal. A height of 14 to 15 inches is about right. This is the approximate height of the seat of most chairs and sofas. A 30-inch length is practical, although you can make the bench up to 6 feet long without changing the basic style.

For a bench 30 inches long, 15 inches high, get a 2 x 12 plank 60 inches long (the top length plus twice the height). Get a 2 x 6 30 inches long (or about the same length as the top) for the cross brace between the legs.

	YOU WILL NEED
Wood	one 2" x 12" plank, 60" long one 2" x 6" plank, 30" long one 16" length of ⅜" doweling
Tools	saw, square, drill and bits, keyhole or sabre saw

Design Sketch of Easy Bench.

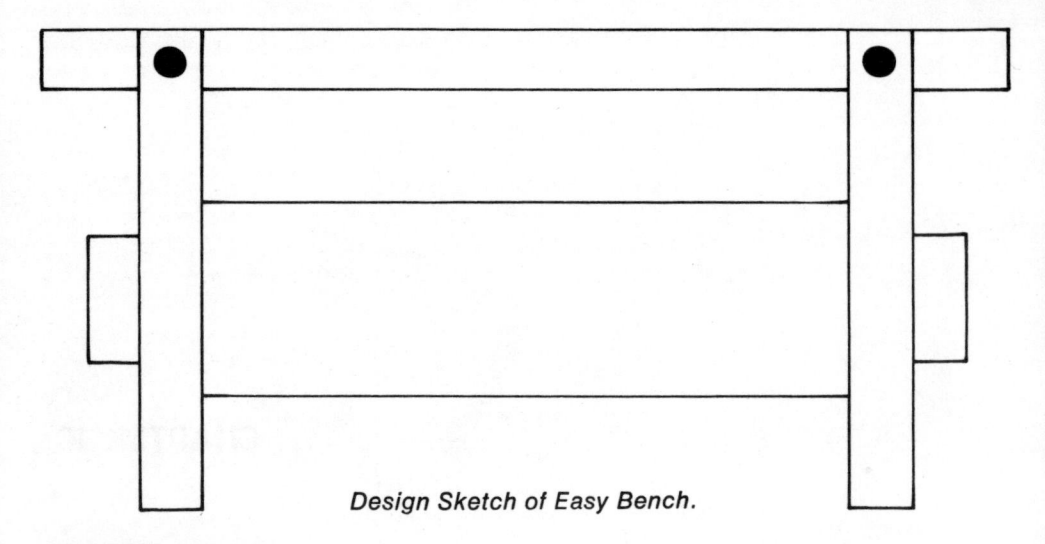

Building Instructions

Start by squaring the ends of the plank. Then, cut off two 15-inch pieces. These cuts must be straight, as they are to be the legs. Measure 3 inches from each corner along the 30-inch tabletop, and mark off the first edge of the slots that the legs will eventually fit into. (Fig. 1.)

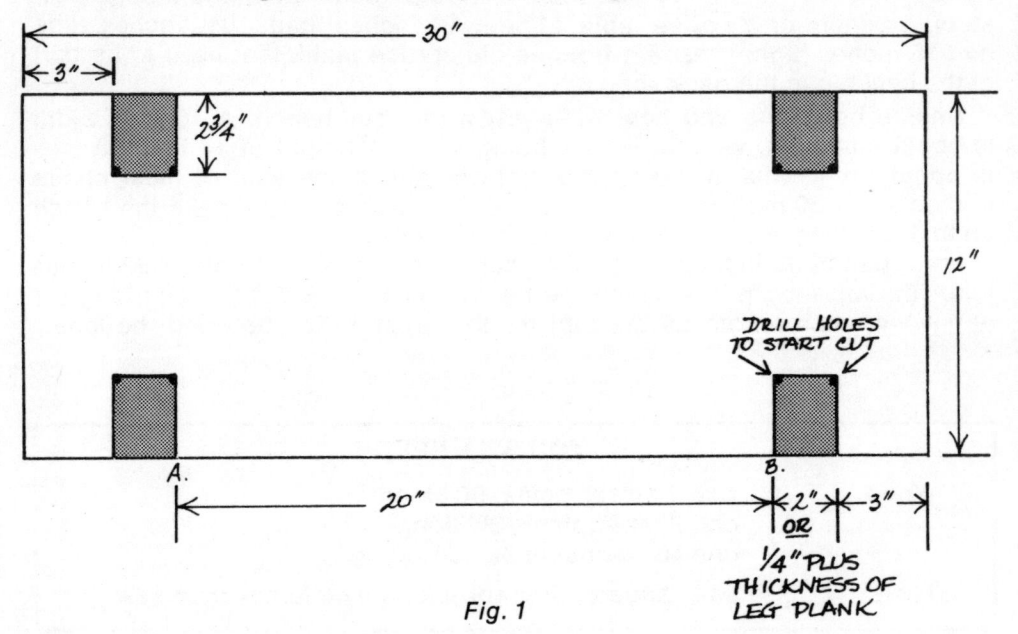

Fig. 1

66

The slots themselves should be cut about ¼ of an inch wider than the thickness of the plank (about 2 inches). They should project 2¾ inches into the plank from the edge.

Do not try to fit the legs into a hole exactly the same size as the tabs. You can do this when you become more experienced but at first allow some extra room for the tabs and slots. It will not detract from the finished look. If you try to be too exact you may have to cut the tabs or slots again. Be careful that your cuts are straight, that they are parallel to each other, and at right angles to the edges. Use a carpenter's square when marking them.

Before cutting the slot, mark the depth by drilling a ¼-inch or ⅜-inch hole at the inner corners of the slots to make the cutting easier. Use your handsaw to make the two cuts to the marking holes, then use the keyhole or coping saw to make the inner cut. (If you are using old wood, the corner pieces may break off. Consult section on old wood, page 15, if it looks as if this might happen.)

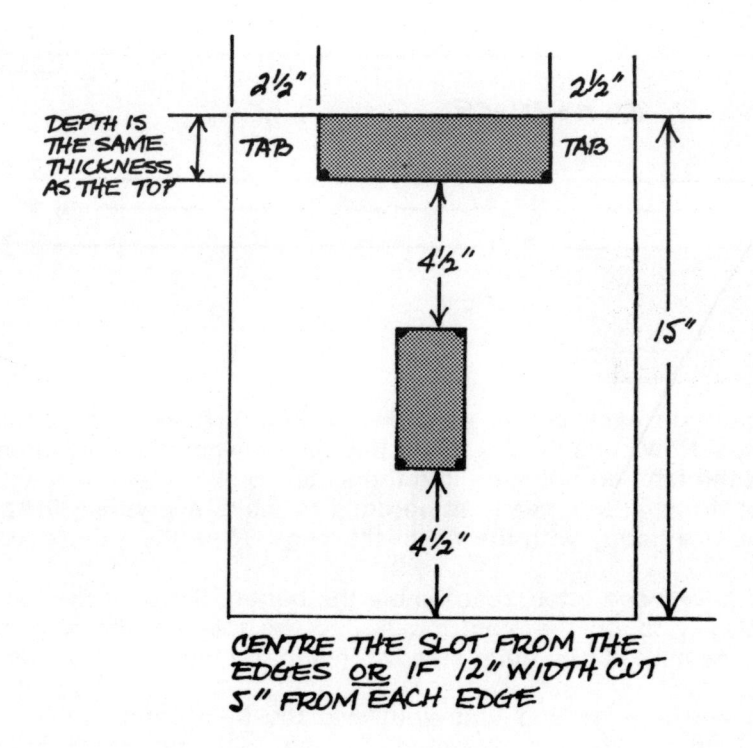

Fig. 2

When the four slots have been prepared, start on the leg pieces.

Cut as shown in Fig. 2, with the depth of the tab the same thickness as the top piece, which is usually 1¾ inches thick for a 2-inch plank. The tabs will be 2½ inches wide. Again, drill a hole at the inner corners to make cutting easier. Center the hole for the 2 x 6 crosspiece. (Fig. 2.) It should measure 2 inches x 4 inches. The lower edge of the hole should be 4½ inches from the bottom of the leg. The top of the hole should be 8½ inches from the bottom of the leg. Center the hole from the edge. For a 12-inch-wide plank, it would be about 5 inches from either edge. (12—2 plank width minus hole width) equals 10, divided by two equals 5.)

Drill a hole in each corner where the slot hole will be and then cut out the slot with your keyhole or sabre saw.

Cut both legs the same.

Now for the 2 x 6. Measure the distance between the slots on one edge of the top (A to B, Fig. 1), and add 8 inches. This will be the desired length of the 2 x 6. Cut at that length.

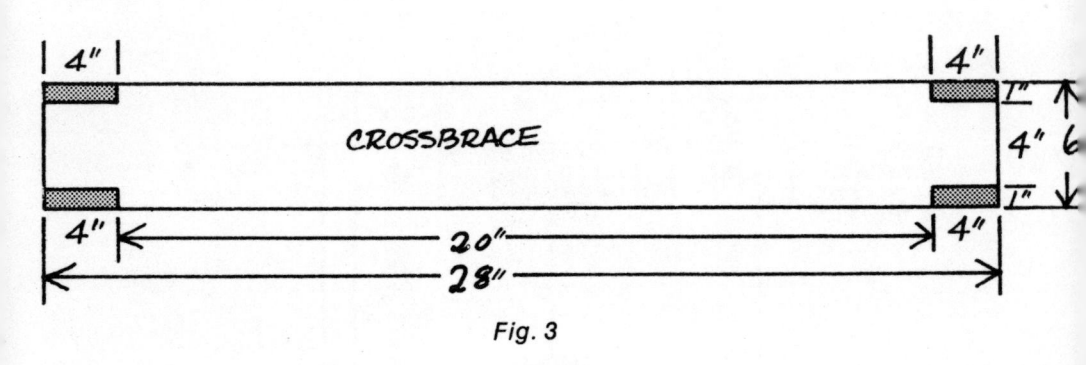

Fig. 3

Cut a 1 x 4 piece off each corner as shown in Fig. 3. Save these small pieces for the pegs. Now slide the 2 x 6 into the slot between the legs, then put the top on. If the tabs do not slide into the slots, you will have to recut, whittle, chisel, or do whatever needs to be done to make everything fit together. When you are happy with the fit, fit the pegs. (See the section on fitting pegs, page 36.)

After the pegs have been fitted, reassemble the bench. Some of the tabs may be sticking up through the slots too far, or the top may be slightly crooked, or the legs may not be quite steady. This is the time to rectify any problems.

Jiggle the top and legs around until you have the best compromise of squareness and flatness. You are now ready for the final step, which is to fasten the top with dowels, although this is not absolutely necessary.

To fasten the top with dowels, drill a hole for the dowel from the edge of the tab through the inner edge of the slot and beyond about 1 inch into the bench top. (Fig. 4.)

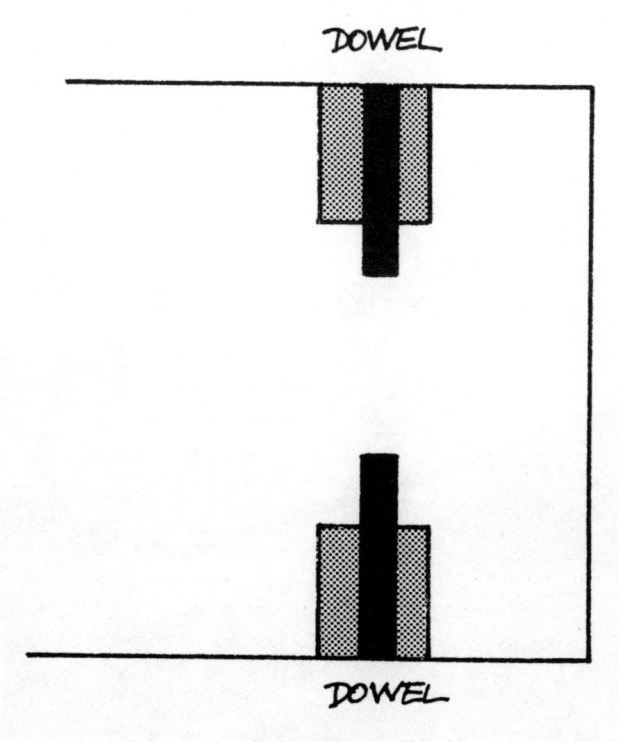

Fig. 4

Cut the dowel to the proper length and tap it into the hole flush with the surface. Do not glue the dowels as you may want to remove them to disassemble the pieces at a later date. Drill a hole and fit a dowel at each tab as you go around the bench top.

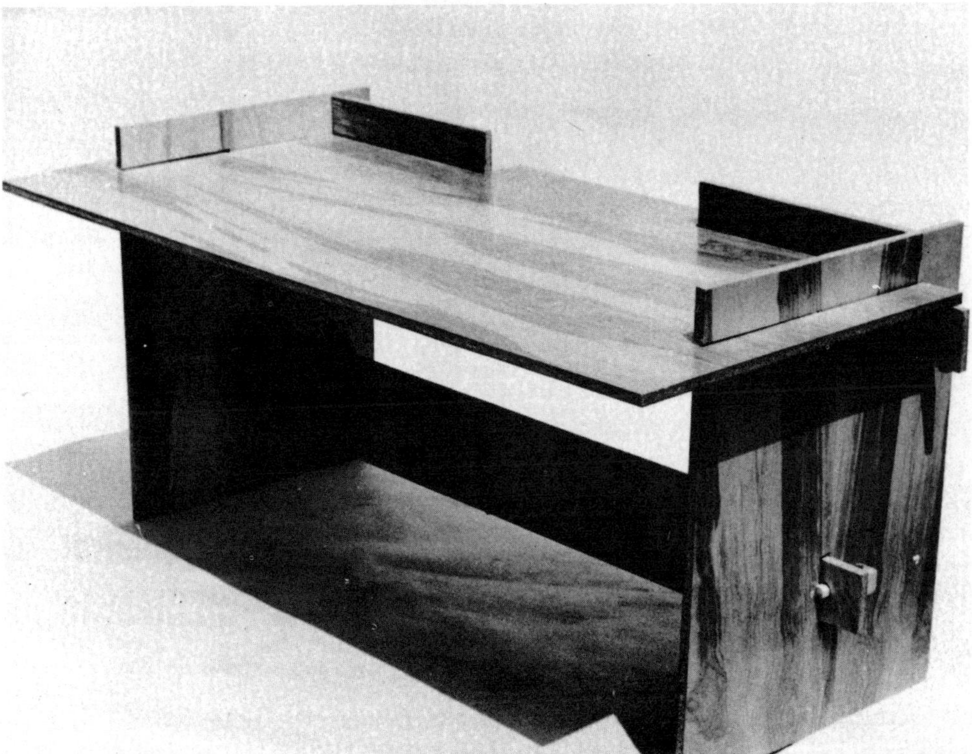

CHAPTER 11

PEGGED DESK

This desk can be built very quickly — you can probably do it in one afternoon. Big, strong, and dependable, it can also be used as a workbench.

The only other material that you might want to use in addition to the sheet of plywood is a scrap of pine or fir to make the four pegs. I get impatient trying to form pegs from plywood because of the laminations, but it is not really all that hard. If you do not have any scraps, you can use dead tree branches about 1 inch in diameter to cut the four 4-inch pegs.

Included are some useful variations on the plain desk. The additions are, of course, more costly and time-consuming.

For a much more attractive piece, get a ¾-inch veneer plateboard. I made a desk with a birch veneer and three coats of urethane satin varnish, and it is really beautiful.

The overall dimensions are 64 x 32 x 32.

	YOU WILL NEED
Wood	one 4' x 8' sheet of ¾" plywood, good-one-side (interior or exterior).
Tools	saw, square, steel tape, keyhole saw, drill and bits.

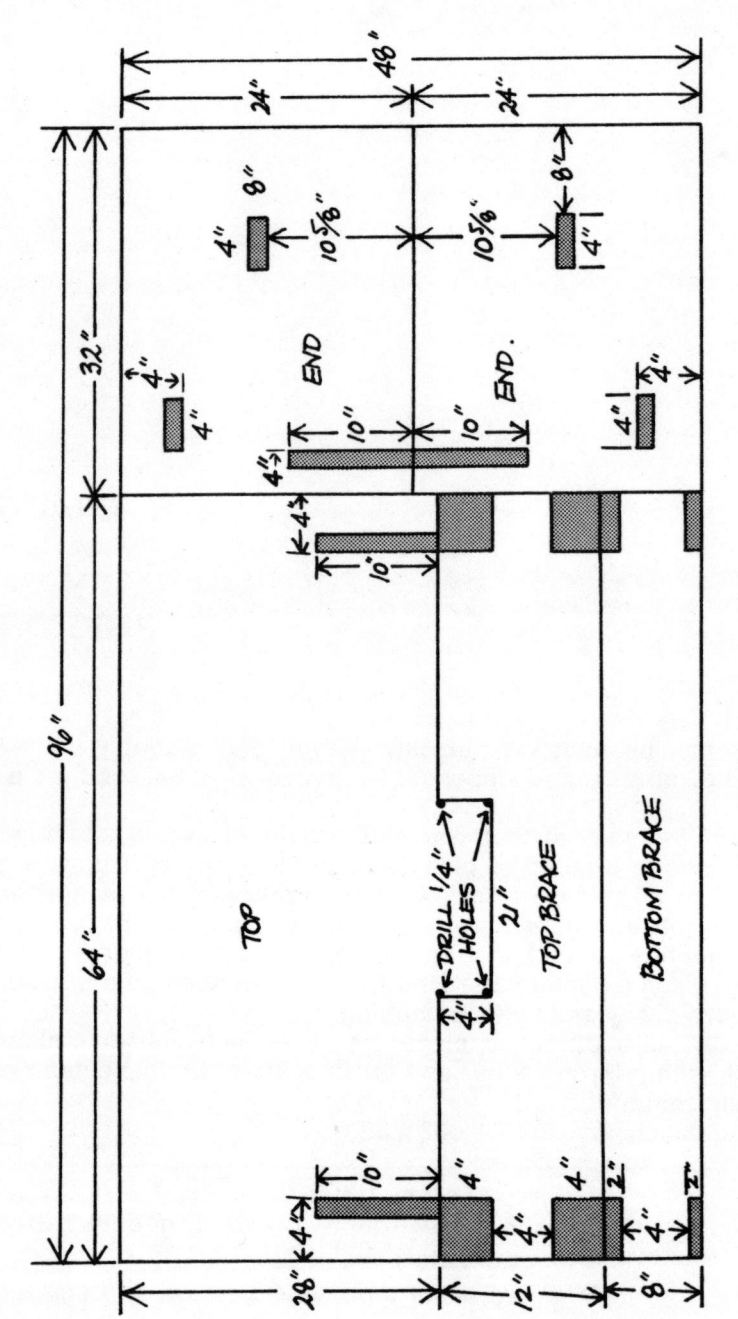

Fig. 1

Building Instructions

Lay out your sheet of plywood or plateboard, with the good side up. Using a carpenter's square and steel tape, mark the sheet as shown in Fig. 1. Check and recheck your measurements before proceeding.

First, cut away from the top the piece that forms the two ends of the desk. Then separate the two ends. Put them aside.

Cut off the lower brace. You now have one more long cut to make — the upper brace from the top. Before you make this cut, drill a ¼-inch hole at the corners as shown in Fig. 1. These small holes will help you start your keyhole saw to make the two 4-inch cuts and the 21-inch cut. Make these cuts. Next, make the 22-inch cuts. You now have all your pieces.

Cut the slots in the end and top pieces. The slots should be approximately ⅞ of an inch wide. Make sure that you cut them properly, as shown in Fig. 1, or, if making the V-shelf, as shown in Fig A. At this point it is easy to get confused, so go slowly.

Cut the tabs on the upper and lower braces.

You can now assemble your desk. Have someone hold the end pieces upright (good side of plywood to the outside). Fit the upper and lower braces into their slots as shown in Fig. 2. Then slide the top on.

See Chapter 5 on fitting pegs.

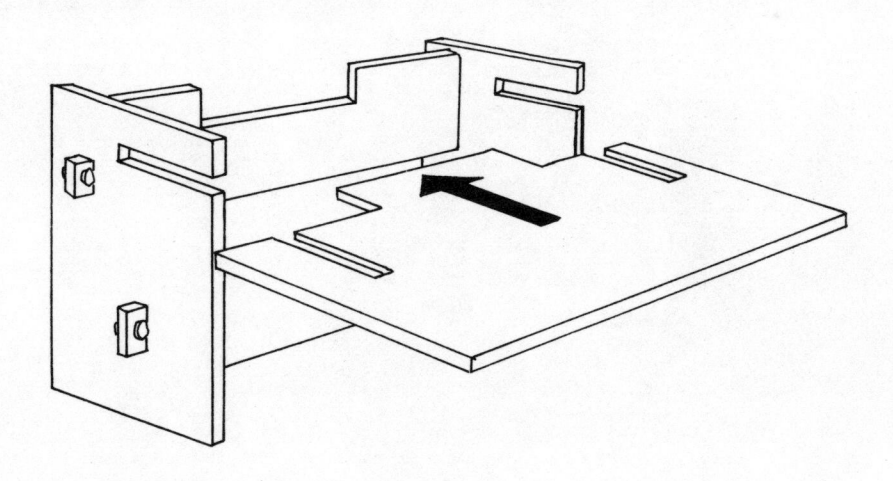

Fig. 2

Inserting the pegs.

Sliding on the top.

Fig. A

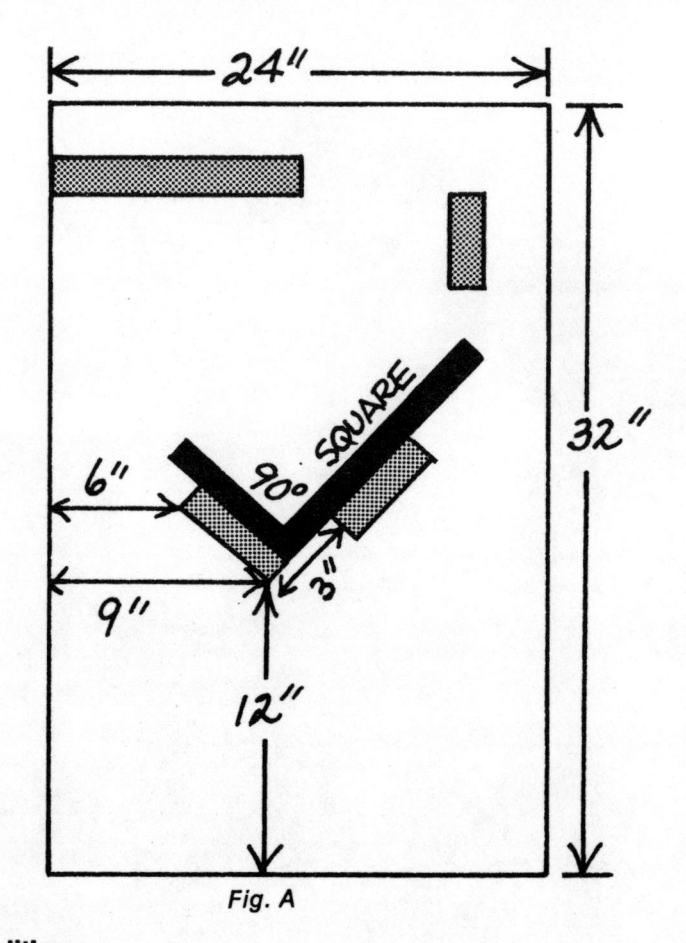

V-Shelf Addition

This shelf runs the length of the desk and is useful for holding books. You will need a 1 x 8 65-inch long sheet, in any wood.

In it cut tabs identical to those in the bottom brace in Fig. 1. Then cut the slots in the ends of the desk as shown in Fig. A. Assemble the desk as before, but with two bottom crosspieces to form your V-shelf, instead of one. You will, of course, need two more pegs to fit into this extra cross brace.

Four-Shelf Addition

For this variation, you will need a piece of plywood 21¼ x 56. Cut as shown in Fig. B. You will also need 22 1-inch angle braces with ⅝-inch screws.

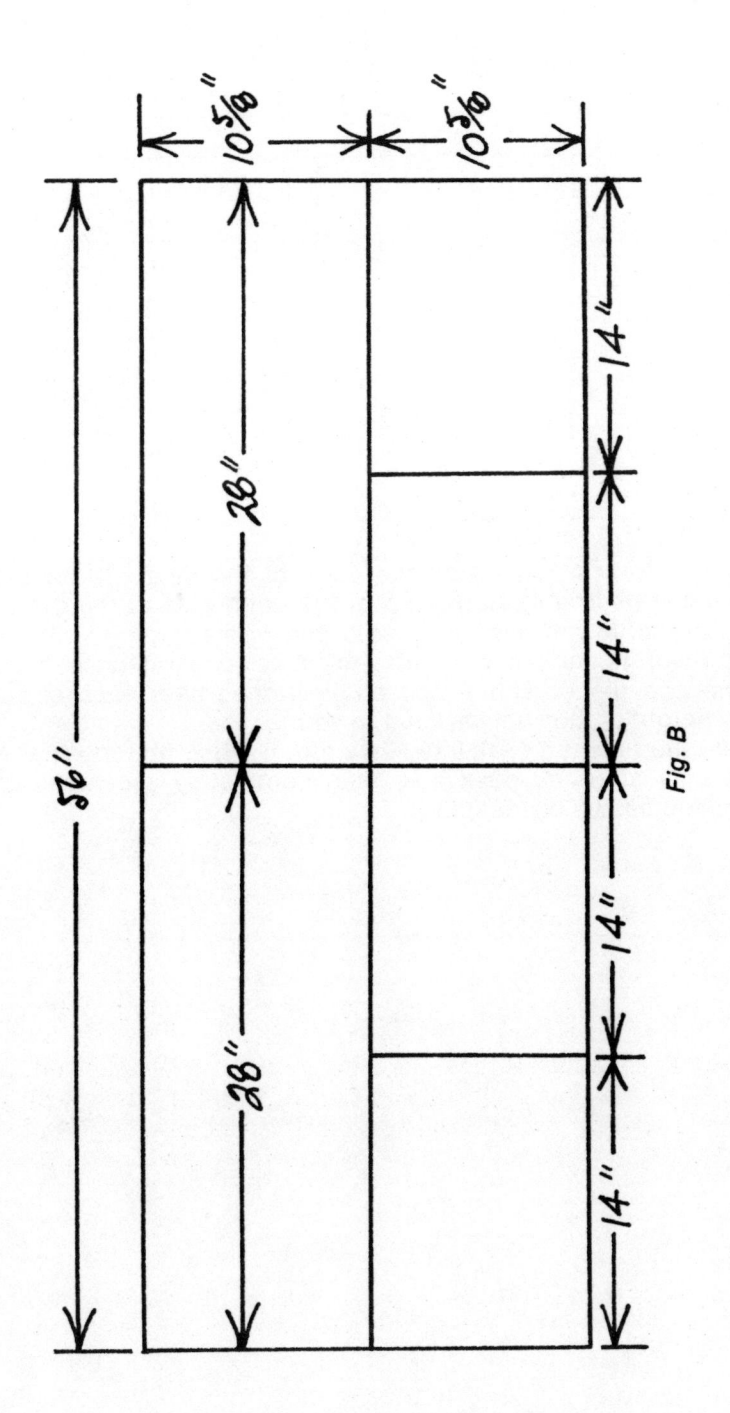

Fig. B

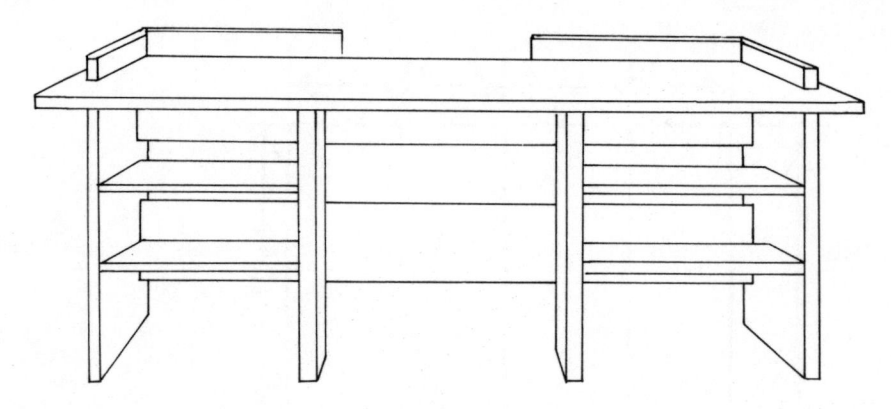

Fig. C

The long pieces form a leg inside the ends of the desk. These are attached with two angles braces to the top of the underside of the desk and, with one angle brace, to the bottom cross brace of the desk.

The shelves (two, 14 inches wide at each side) are attached between this leg and the end piece, with 1-inch angle braces near each corner of each shelf. The height of the shelves is up to you.

From the front the finished desk looks like Fig. C. Note that these shelves can be added only after the desk has been completely assembled. They have to be removed before dismantling.

CHAPTER 12

QUICK-AND-EASY KITCHEN TABLE

This well designed table is ideal for either eating or working. It is quickly and easily constructed, and comes apart simply by removing two pegs and a few screws.

Use good-one-side plywood, or veneer plateboard. Two pieces of veneer taping 8 feet long will cover the edges around the tabletop. Use contact cement for applying the taping.

You can sculpt the shape of the legs into whatever shape you desire, but leave them 24 inches wide at the top and bottom. Plywood is strong, but do not cut away too much when sculpting the legs. Eight inches is the maximum. If your floors are crooked, the table might rock a bit. To correct this, work on the underside of each leg and carve out a semicircle starting about 3 inches in from each edge. (Fig. 1.)

	YOU WILL NEED
Material	one ¾" x 4' x 6' sheet of plywood or plateboard
	four 3" angle braces and 16 ⅝" No. 8 flat-head wood screws
	contact cement
	two 8'-long pieces of veneer taping (optional)
Tools	saw, square, steel tape, drill and bits, keyhole saw, hammer, and screwdriver

There is very little wastage of lumber when making the Quick-and-Easy Kitchen Table. One 4 x 6 sheet of plywood or plateboard is all that is needed. This table is ideal both for the kitchen or the workshop.

Quick-and-Easy Kitchen Table.

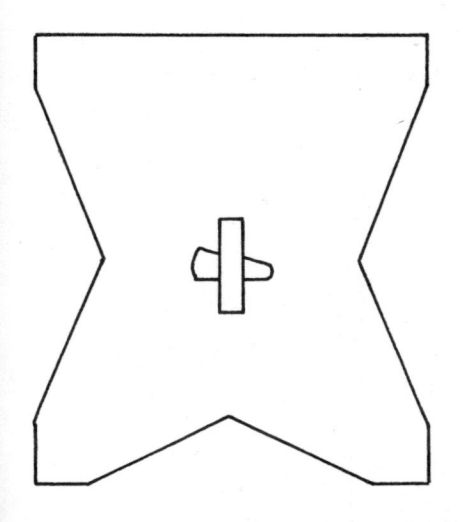

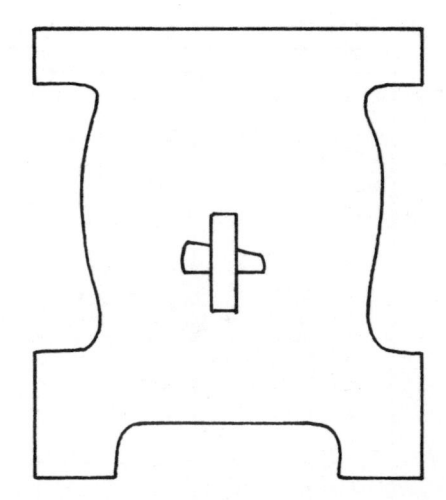

Fig. 1

Building Instructions

These instructions are for a 6-foot sheet of plywood. You can use an 8-foot sheet, simply by making the tabletop and brace longer and leaving the legs as they are. I chose a 6-foot length, as basically, this is a light-duty table suitable for 4 people. If longer, the top might have to be reinforced to keep it from sagging. A couple of 2 x 2s glued and nailed on to the underside, running along the length of the top between the legs work well as reinforcements.

Mark and cut the sheet of wood as shown in Fig. 2. Shape the legs as, and if desired, but be sure to mark the slot in the legs before sculpting.

Cut the slots into the legs as shown in Fig. 2. Cut the tabs for the brace. See Chapter 5 on fitting pegs.

When the tabs and slots in the legs and the cross braces have been cut, assemble these pieces and insert the pegs. They should stand up by themselves.

Set the top on the legs, centering it so that the end and side overhangs are equal.

Make a pencil line along the underside of the top where it touches the inside of the legs. Make this mark on both ends. Attach the 3-inch angle braces to the legs 3 inches in from the edge of the leg at all 4 places. The

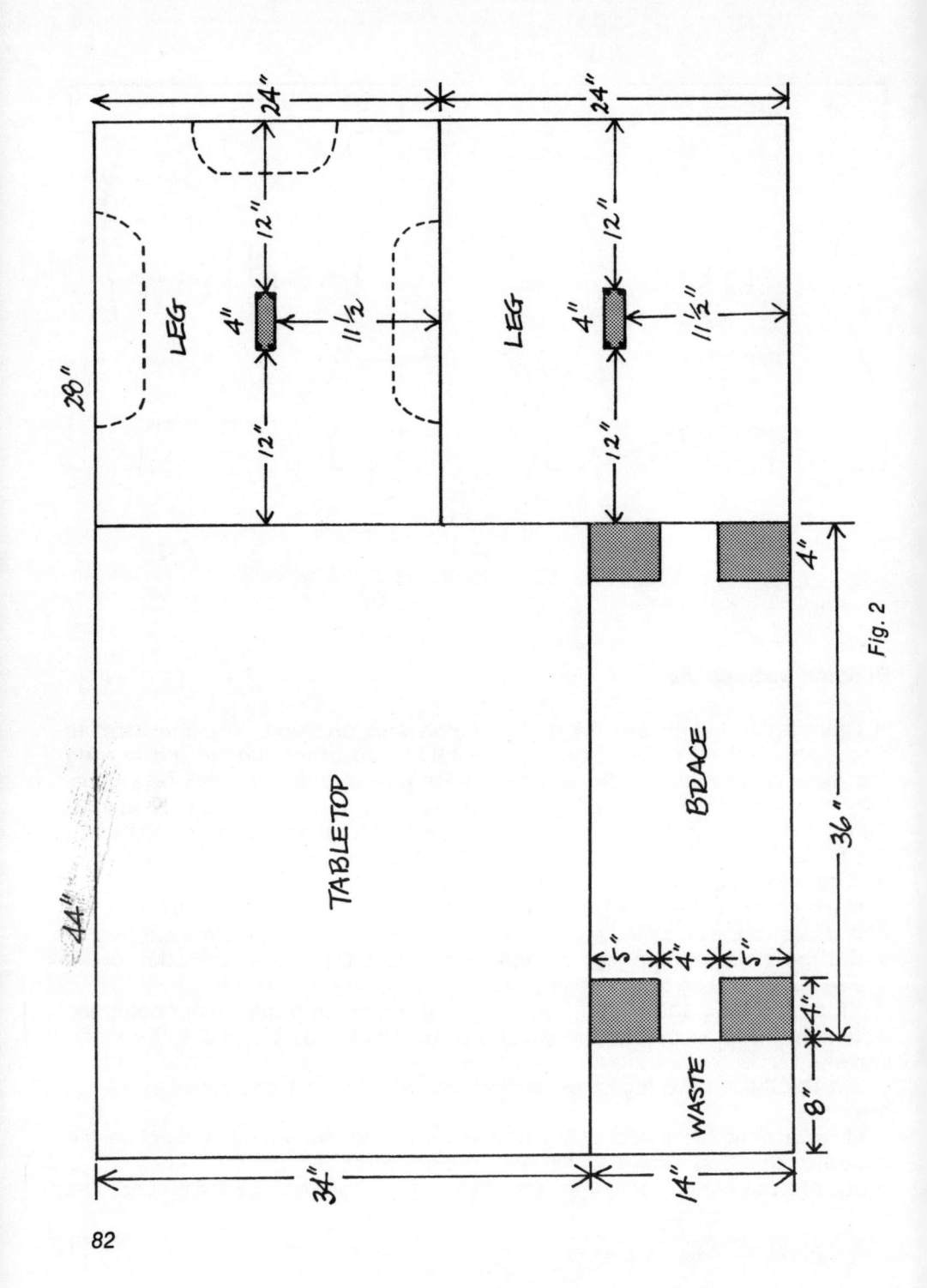

Fig. 2

Fig. 3

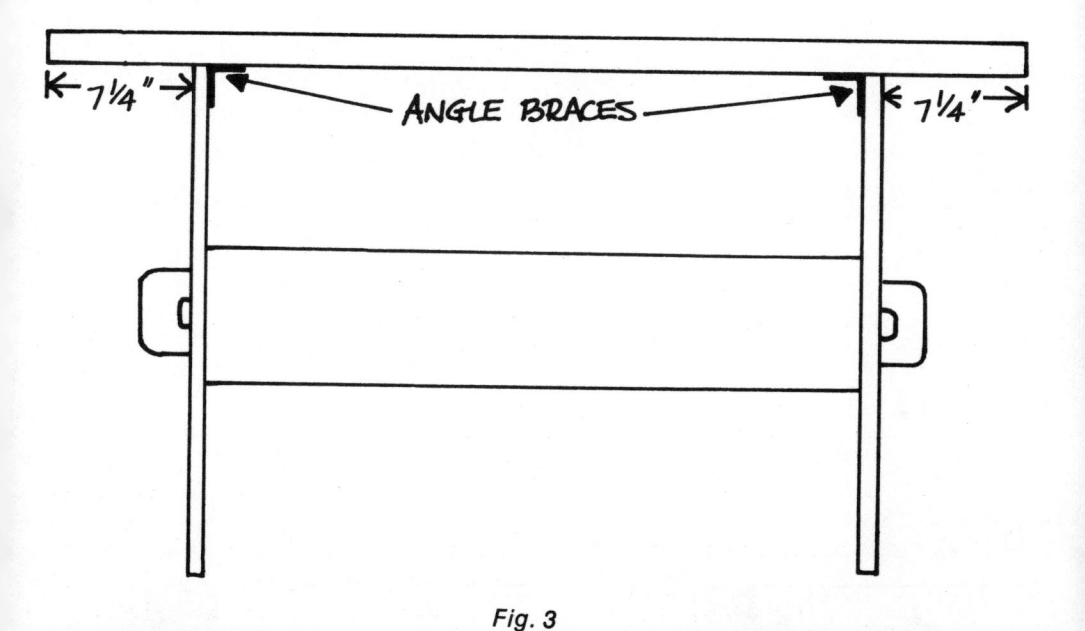

angle braces should be on the inner side of the legs. Drill pilot holes for the screws. (Fig. 3.)

When all four angle braces have been attached, check the pencil marks to make sure that the top has not moved. Drill the pilot holes for the screws into the top and attach.

Cut the veneer taping to length for the edges of the tabletop, and attach with contact cement. Trim as needed.

Fig. 1

CHAPTER 13

FULL-WALL BOOKCASE

This is a very easy and quickly built full-wall shelving unit, also useful as a room-divider. Use your imagination as to the overhang of the shelves and shelf height; you will be more than happy with the results. As with the other plans, this can be easily dismantled and moved. Read the directions and study the diagrams. Then decide how you want your unit to look.

	YOU WILL NEED
Wood	1½" dowels
	1" x 10" boards
	⅜" doweling
Hardware	2" angle braces with four screws each, two for each 1½" dowel
Tools	saw, square, drill, hole saw, or expanding wood bit to fit drill

Planning

The 1½ inch dowels should be the height of your ceiling. Dowels can sometimes be acquired free from carpet dealers, as carpets come rolled up on them. They are also sold at lumberyards or building-supply stores as stairway bannisters.

The boards can be pine, spruce, fir, or any other soft wood. If you plan to put books or other heavy articles on the shelves, there should be no more than about 36 inches between the upright dowels. For lighter articles, 48 inches between the upright dowels is the maximum length.

The 1½-inch dowels go right through the boards, hence you can make the shelving interesting by using a variety of overhangs.

For example, the overall length of the shelf boards could be: 12-inch overhang plus 40" for the main shelf plus 3" overhang, for a total of 55 inches. Drill dowel hole at each end of the 40-inch measurement. (Fig. 3.)

Decide how much wall space you want covered, study Fig. 1, and choose your own measurements. For a heavily weighted unit, use two upright dowels for each shelf end, otherwise one per shelf end will do.

To plan the height between the shelves, measure the height of whatever you plan to put on them, adding 1 inch to each space to allow for the thickness of the board. For example, for a 12-inch shelf space, allow 13 inches. Again, plan a variety of heights. Allow some extra room, as shelves look cramped when close together.

To reduce complications, and to adjust the height of the shelves, drill holes for the cross pins (for holding the shelves up) at 6 or 8-inch intervals on the upright dowels. Study Fig. 1, decide how many tiers you would like, how many shelves per tier, the length of the shelves, and the number of overhangs. Make a sketch of the unit.

From your sketch, figure out how many boards and dowels you will need. Assemble the materials. You will need one piece of ⅜-inch doweling for each upright where each shelf crosses it. That is, 4 4-inch dowel cross-

Fig. 2

pieces for each shelf, if you have two upright dowels for each shelf end. You will also need a 2-inch corner brace for each end of each upright dowel to anchor the uprights both to the floor and to either the ceiling or the upper wall. (Fig. 4.)

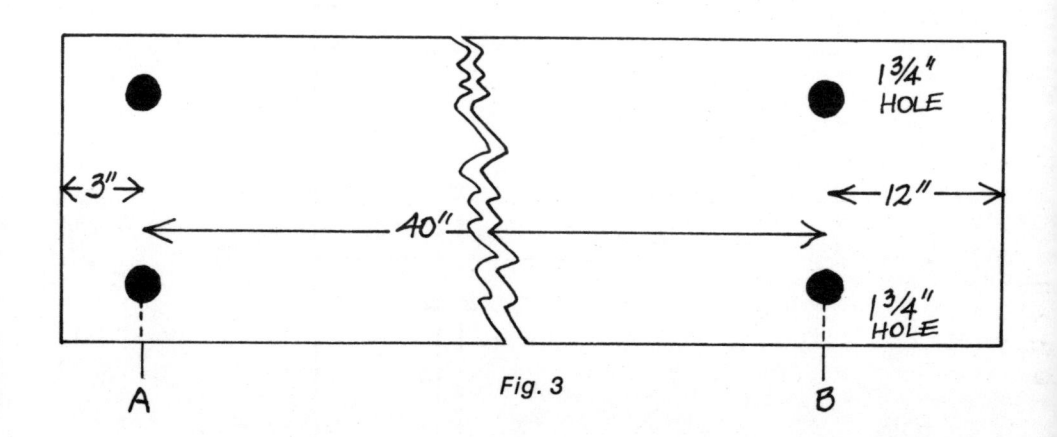

Fig. 3

Cutting

Begin by cutting the upright dowels into lengths to suit your ceiling height. Next mark a straight line up the side of the upright along which to drill the holes for the ⅜-inch cross pins. Lay the dowel alongside the board and mark along the board with a pencil for the full length of the dowel. (Fig. 2.)

Mark a crosshatch on the long line on the upright dowels where you will drill the hole for the cross pins (your sketch shows the distance between your shelves).

Measure all the uprights from the bottom to the top. This is to ensure that the shelves will be level when the unit is standing. Using a steel tape, mark the crosshatches exactly the same for all uprights that pass through the same shelf.

Use a ⅜-inch drill for the ⅜-inch dowel cross pins. Drill the holes **straight** through the upright dowels. If these holes are crooked, your shelves will be crooked.

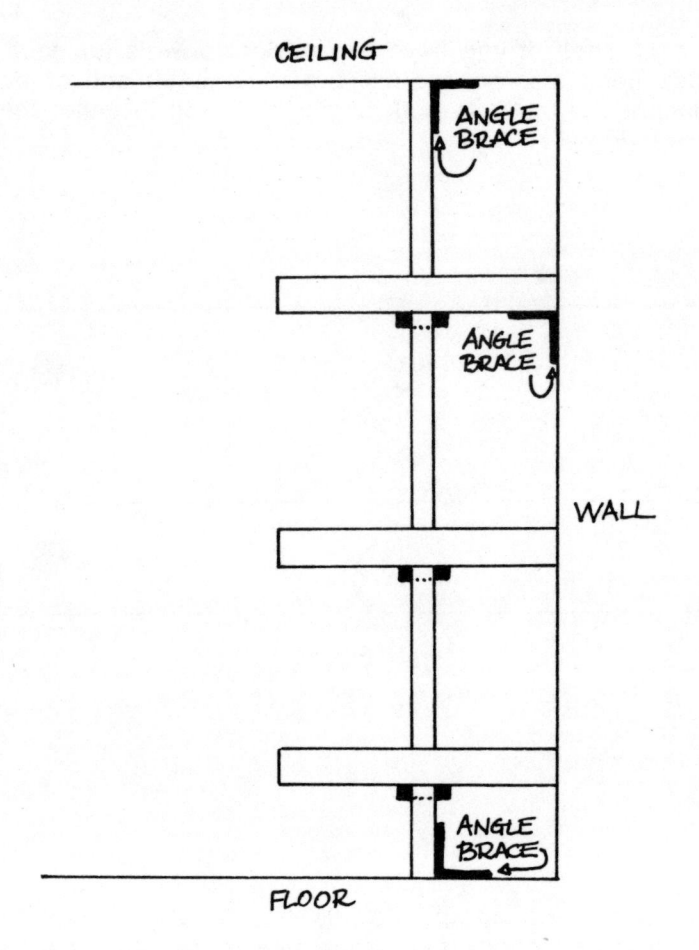

Fig. 4

Next, cut your shelf boards to the desired length. Now mark the holes for the upright dowels that the shelf boards will slide over. To make the holes, you need either a hole saw or an expanding wood bit for your drill. Either one will make the 1¾-inch hole, and both are available at any hardware store for about $2.00. (Fig. 3.)

Mark your boards as shown in Fig. 3 with whatever combination of overhang you have decided upon. When marking the boards, make sure that the length between the dowel holes is always the same, that is, as in point A to point B in Fig. 3. If you measure in from each end of the board to mark your holes, they may be off a bit. Double check by measuring between the marks for the holes.

Cut your ⅜-inch doweling into 4-inch pieces. You will need 4 for every shelf board when using 2 upright dowels per shelf end. You will need only 2 cross pins per shelf board when using one upright dowel for each shelf end.

If you are going to put a finish on the unit, it is easiest to do it now. After the whole piece has been assembled, it will be difficult to work around the dowels. Shelves do not **have** to be finished; they are quite attractive left as they are.

When you are ready to put the shelf unit up, get some friends to help. Slide all the shelf boards, in their proper sequence, to their proper places on the upright dowels, and insert the cross pins below each shelf. When the unit has been completely assembled, raise it to the ceiling, and anchor it there with the corner braces. If it is more convenient, the top shelf can be anchored to the wall instead of anchoring the uprights to the ceiling. (Fig. 4.)

The finished unit must stand either directly upright or lean slightly against the wall — not into the room.

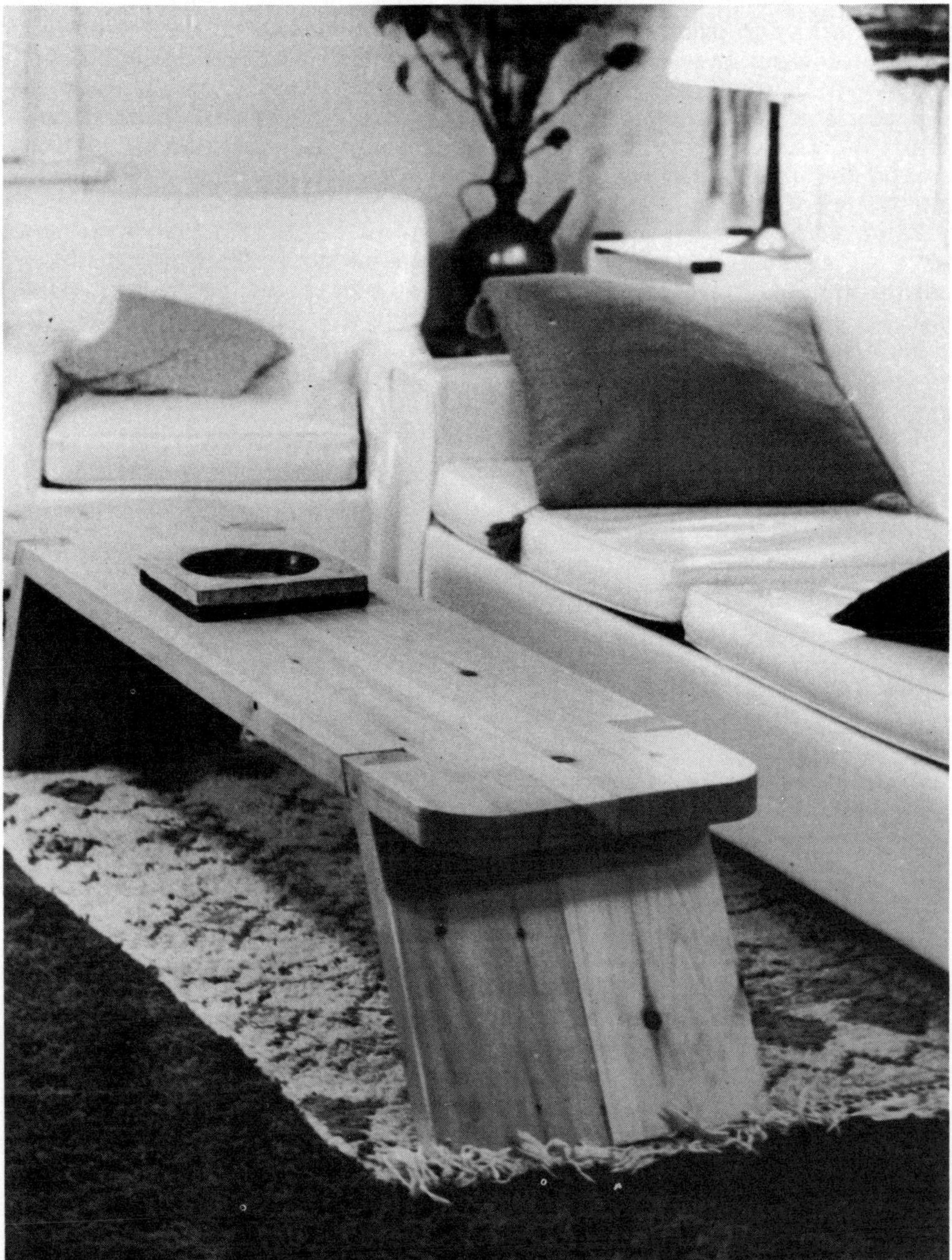

CHAPTER 14

CLASSIC COFFEE TABLE

Great as either a coffee table or bench, this design is very strong. I have had as many as four people sitting on mine at one time. It is extremely attractive and fits well with almost anything. The tabletop is 61 inches long when cut from an 8-foot plank. If this is too long, get a shorter plank. The tabletop here is 35 inches shorter than the total length of the plank and stands 16 inches off the floor.

I specify a 2 x 14 plank. This may be hard to find, as many lumberyards carry planks up to only 12-inch widths. A 12-inch width is fine for a bench, but it may be a bit narrow for a coffee table. Look at a 12-inch plank and decide for yourself. If you want a wider top, and cannot get a 14-inch plank, buy two 2 x 8s, 8 feet long and join them together. (See section on joining narrow planks, page 30.)

	YOU WILL NEED
Wood	one 2" x 14" 8' long pine, cedar, fir, or any soft wood plank (or two 2" x 8" 8' planks)
	four ⅜" dowels 4" long
Tools	protractor or a 30°-60°-90° triangle, saw, carpenter's square, keyhole or coping saw, drill and ⅜" wood bit

Building Instructions

Square the ends of your plank, then cut off one 35-inch length. Eighteen inches from one end of this 35-inch piece, mark a 60° angle on the edge with the mark slanting towards the end you measured from. (Fig. 1.)

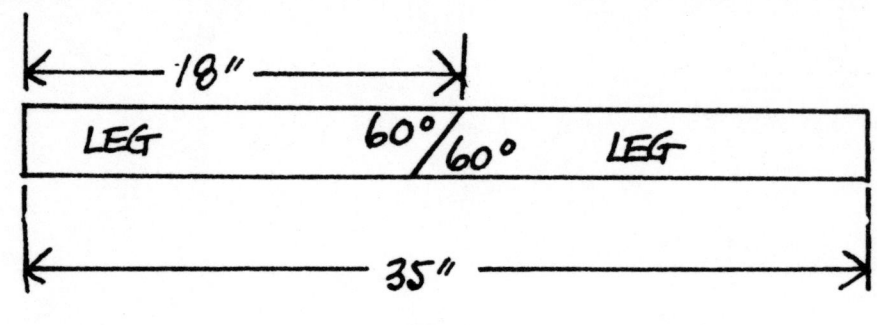

Fig. 1

If you are using a handsaw (as I do), you can make these angle cuts easily by marking both sides of the board across the width of the board at the place where you want your saw to cut. Next, make the cut with the plank on its edge, watching the saw cuts along the mark on both sides. Extra hands to hold the plank are helpful. It is, of course, easier to make the angle cuts with a power saw set to cut at the correct angle. Try to cut straight, as these are your legs. After you have made the cut, lay these two pieces aside.

Next, the long piece. Decide which of the two surfaces you want for the top. Then lay it face up and measure 8 inches in from each end, making a mark across the tabletop using your square. (Fig. 3.) Tip the plank up on its edge and mark as shown in Fig. 2. The leg slots will be at a 60° angle. The slots will be just wider (about ¼ of an inch) than the thickness of the two leg pieces (about 2 inches as most 2-inch planks are actually 1¾ inches thick), but check your plank to make sure that you are marking it right. All lines must be parallel.

Mark your plank as shown in Fig. 3, with the slots going in 3 inches from the edge, 2 inches wide. Make these cuts on the 60-degree angle, cutting in from the edge of the plank. Cut the inner side of the slot with a coping saw or keyhole saw.

If your plank shows signs of splitting along an existing crack, repair it. See the section on repairing old wood, page 17.

Now mark the two leg pieces as shown in Fig. 4. Notice that you will be cutting the tabs out on the end that is cut off square. (The end cut at an angle is the floor end of the leg). The two pieces are exactly the same and

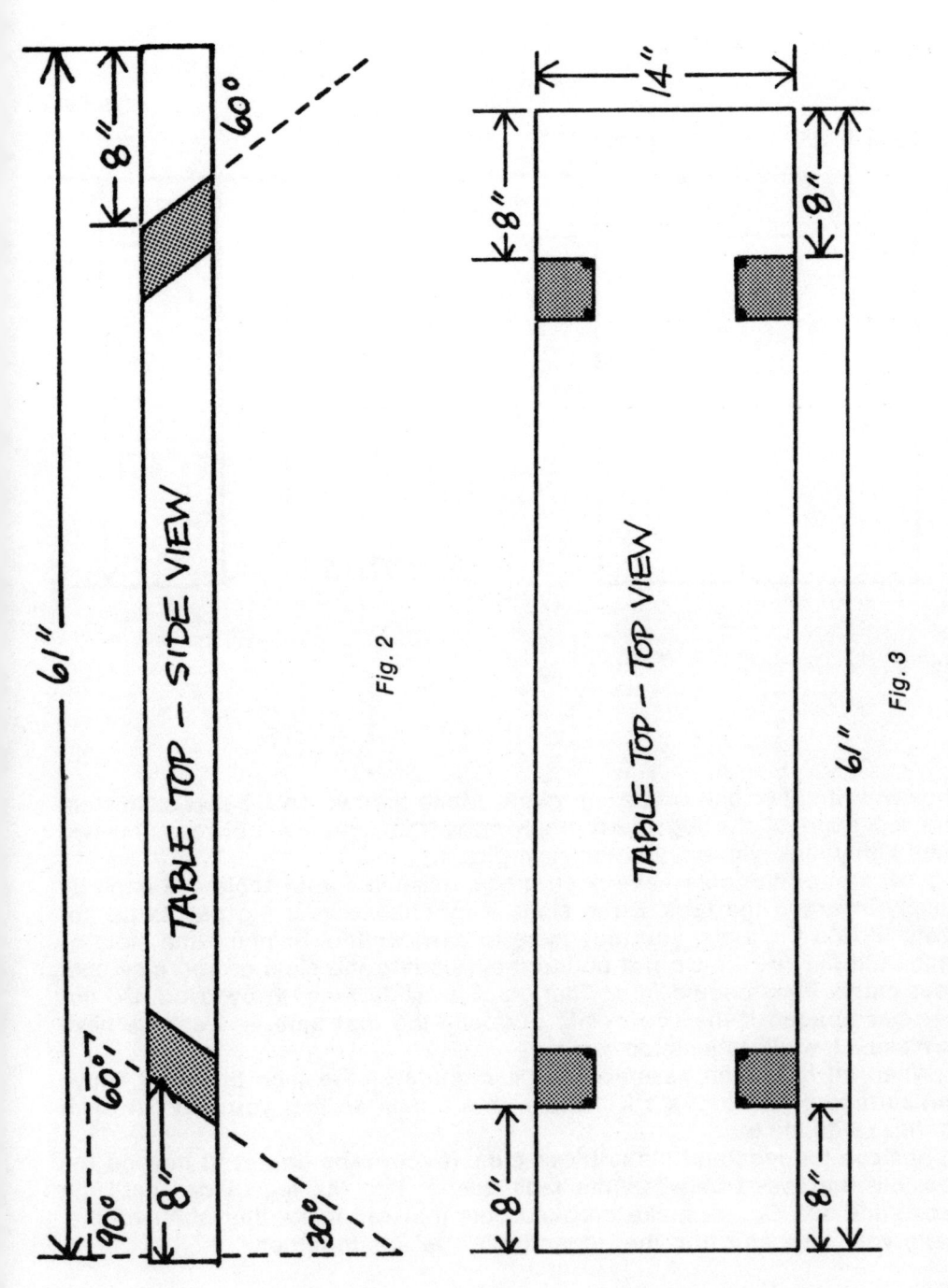

Fig. 2

Fig. 3

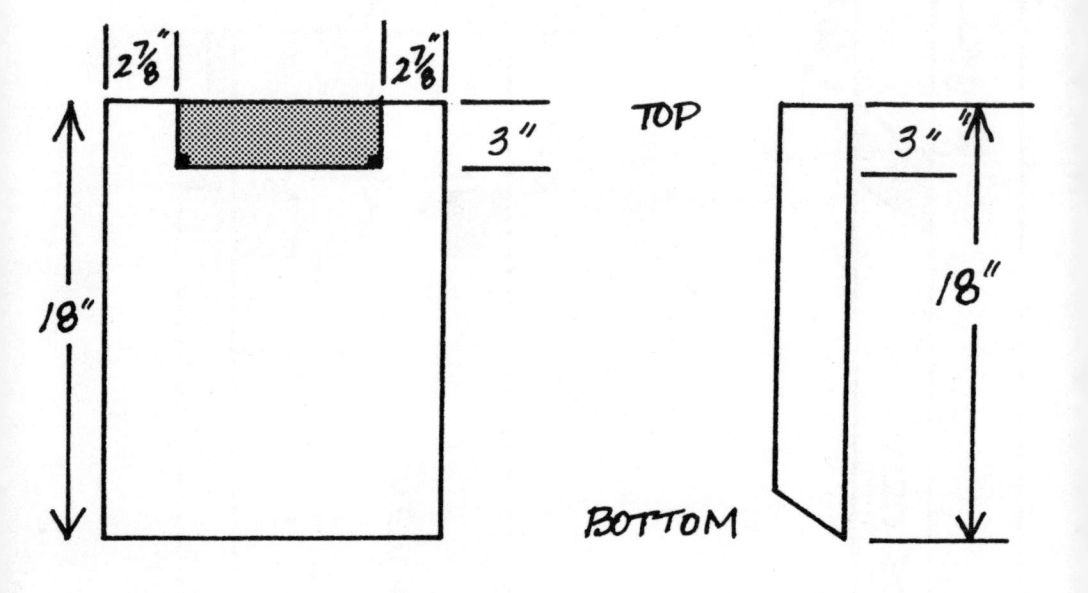

Fig. 4

they will fit either end of the top plank. Make the two cuts 3 inches in from the top edge of the leg plank, then make the long cut between the two tabs with your keyhole or coping saw. (Fig. 4.)

Now that all the cuts have been made, assemble your table or bench by simply inserting the tabs in the slots. If by chance your leg pieces do not quite fit into the slots, you may have to saw, whittle, or plane the slots or tabs until they do fit. Do not pound the tabs into the slots or you may split your plank. They should fit so that you can slide them in by hand. Do not get discouraged if they do not fit perfectly the first time — I always have to make a few alterations too.

When all has been assembled, the corners of the tabs protrude above the surface of the top. Mark these with a pencil so that you can cut them off flush with the top.

Remove the legs and make these cuts. If your tabs do not fit beyond the top, cut the space between the tabs deeper into the leg pieces until the tabs stick out. Do not make crooked cuts that will make the table wobble. Take your time and trim the edges until it all fits together.

Now that your table is finished, you will notice that when you lift it up, the legs fall out! This may be handy for moving, but not for housecleaning. To prevent the legs from falling out, drill a ⅜-inch hole through the tab and about 1 inch into the top piece. Fit a ⅜-inch dowel into these holes.

Do not attempt to nail through the tab, or you will surely split it. You could use a long screw instead of the dowel, but drill a hole through the tab for the screw first.

Pages 96 to 104 show, step by step, how to make the Classic Coffee Table.

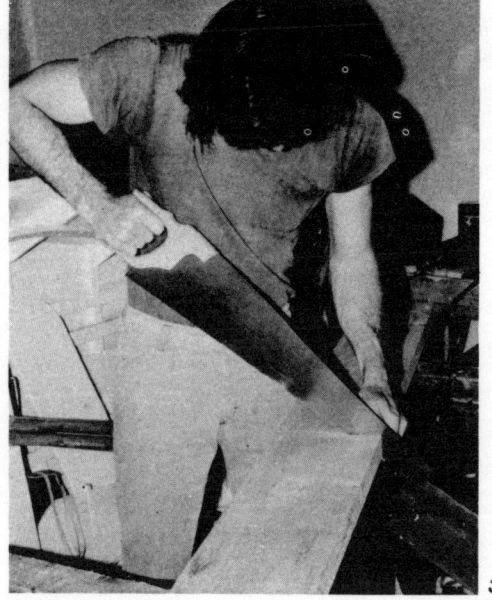

1. Carrying home the two 2 x 8 seven-foot-long white pine planks from the local lumberyard.

2. Square the ends of the planks to get a straight end, cutting off any splits or bad knots at the ends.

3. Cut each plank into two pieces — one pair 35" long for the legs (to be cut again later after joining). The other plank pair is for the coffee tabletop.

4.

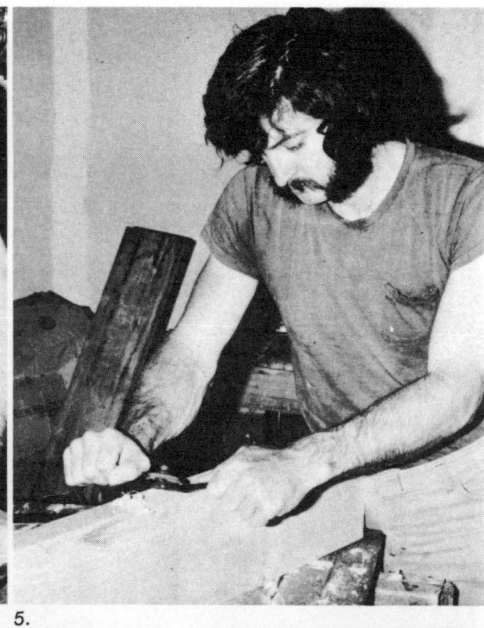

5.

4. Lay the first set of planks to be joined together side-by-side to determine how they best fit together.

5. Plane down any high spots that prevent the planks from lying tightly together.

6. Mark the places for the dowels across the plank edges using the carpenter's square. I marked them about 8" apart.

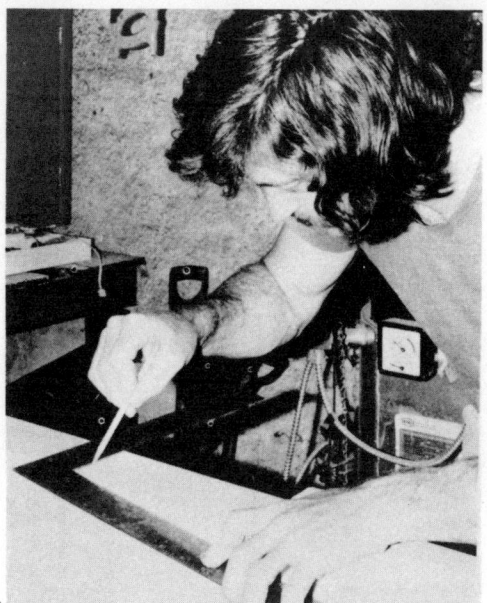

6.

7. 8.

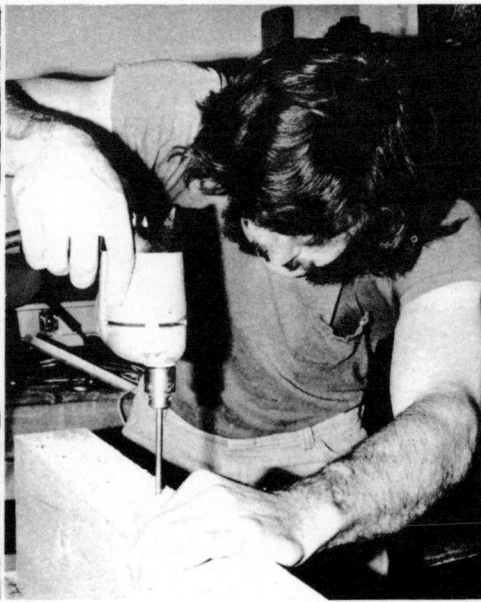

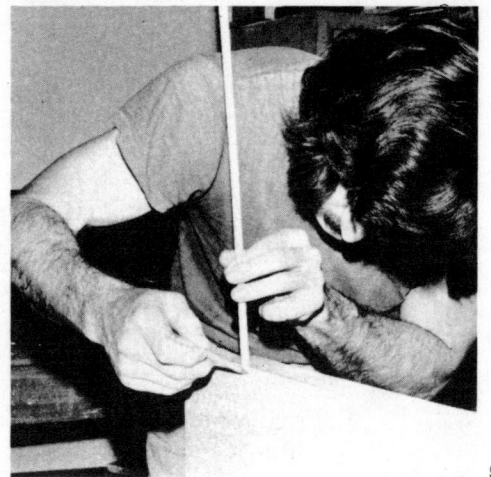

9.

7. Mark the crosshatch for the dowels on the lines shown in photo 6, using a wooden block. The block, in this case, is ¾" thick. I hold it flush with the outer edges and mark along it.

8. Drill the holes at the crosshatches. I am using a ⅜" drill bit for ⅜" diameter doweling. Remove the shavings after the holes are drilled. Be sure the holes are straight and that all are approximately the same 2" depth.

9. Mark the depth of the hole with the doweling. If the holes are 2" deep in each plank, I cut the dowels 3½" long. This allows an extra ½" in case there are excess shavings in the holes.

10.

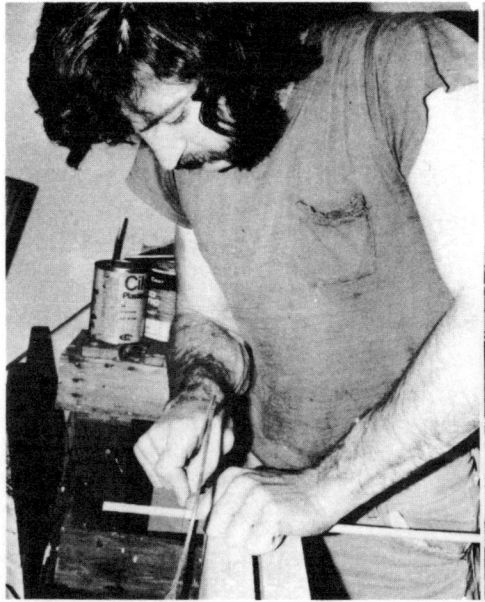

11.

10. Cut the dowels all the same length. A fine-toothed saw, such as a coping saw, will cut the doweling more easily than the crosscut saw.

11. Put a few drops of glue in each of the dowel holes and a few drops around each dowel before inserting it partway into the holes.

12. Insert all the dowels in the holes on the same plank edge. Run a generous zig-zag bead of glue along the edge of one of the planks.

12.

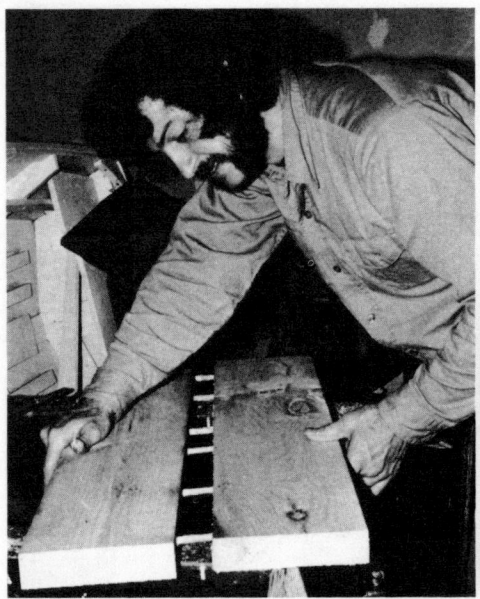

13. When all the dowels are ready insert them into the other plank and push them together as tight as possible.

14. Tip the planks on edge and pound on a piece of wood lying along the edge of the planks. Pound on the planks in several places along the edge. This will ensure a good tight joint.

15. Put the *plank* in the clamps immediately. There should be one clamp near each end of the planks. Insert the buffer block between the wedge and the plank edge and drive the wedge tight with a hammer.

16. Check to see that the plank edges are together and wipe off the excess glue, making sure that the joint between the planks is, however, filled with glue. (Add more glue if necessary.)

17. Mark and cut the slots in the tabletop as in the building plans in Chapter 14. Make the angle cuts in from the edge using your crosscut saw.

18. Make the inner cuts with a coping saw. Start the cuts with the coping saw by turning the blade in the handle to cut around the corner. If you are using a keyhole or sabre saw, you may have to drill a hole to start this cut.

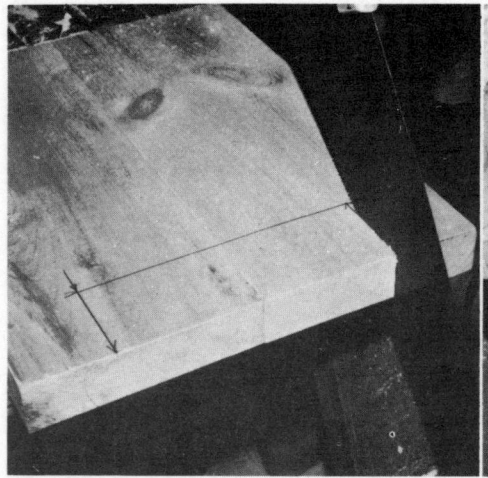

19. Having cut the 35" pieces on an angle for the legs as described in Chapter 14 (with the crosscut saw, as for cutting the slots in photo 17), mark and cut the tabs in the legs as per the building plans in Chapter 14. The tabs will be on the end that is cut off square, not the angle cut end.

20. Make the inner cut with your coping saw, keyhole saw, or, as above with your sabre saw. This is a straight cut, not on an angle.

21. Insert the leg tabs into the slots on the tabletop. The corners will project beyond the tabletop. Do not force the tabs into the slots. Trim the tabs or the slots to make them fit easily. NOTE: be sure that you push the bottom of the legs to the outside of the table as far as they will go. This will make the tabs bind in the slots, ensuring that the legs are rigid.

22. With a pencil, mark around the tabs where they project beyond the tabletop.

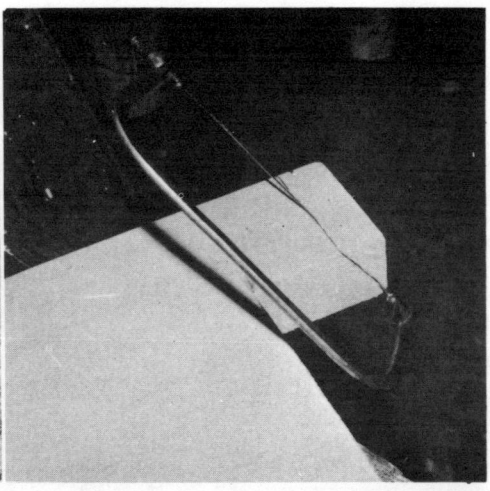

23. Cut the tabs off at the pencil marks. Your coping or keyhole saw will be easier to manage than your crosscut saw when making these cuts.

24. Sand the table, first using coarse, then medium, then fine sandpaper. Sand the plank ends heavily to expose the cross grain and to eliminate the saw marks.

25.

26.

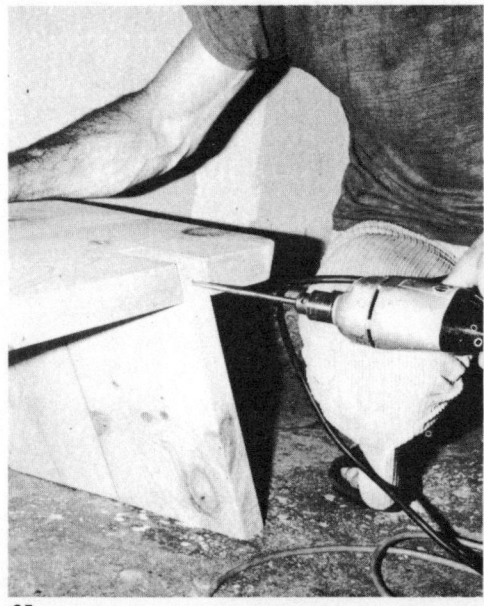

27.

25. When the table pieces have been sanded, assemble the table and drill holes for the dowels that will hold the legs on. Drill straight through the tab and about 2" into the tabletop. Cut a dowel that will fit flush in the hole.

26. I am using a satin urethane varnish. Put on a heavy first coat, really soaking the urethane into the wood.

27. Lightly sand the table between coats of varnish with very fine (220 grit) sandpaper. This will help give you a very smooth finish. I usually apply three coats of varnish. If your finish is slightly rough after the last coat of varnish, you may sand it again lightly, but be sure the varnish is dry. Also only sand with the grain and do it lightly.

CHAPTER 15

TAB-AND-SLOT BENCH

This design is one of my favorites. On my bench I put a 1-inch thick foam pad, covered with an India-block print, and it looks quite spectacular.

The bench can be made with ¾-inch plywood instead of the wide board, but the grain of a wide board is much more attractive. If you want to use plywood, see the Two-From-One Bench, page 111, for some minor adjustments. (For example, the cross brace fits against the top to keep it from sagging. Thus the cross-brace slot is in a different position on the ends.)

Check used lumber places for wide boards if you cannot get new wood, or, join narrow boards — see section on joining narrow planks, page 30.

The bench should be about 16 inches wide to maintain its effect, but you can, however, scale the size to whatever wood you want to use. This design is 16 inches high and 58 inches long.

	YOU WILL NEED
Wood	one 1" x 18" 8' long pine, cedar, fir, any soft wood or ¾" plywood board
	one 2" x 6" 58" long pine, cedar, fir, spruce, any soft wood plank
Tools	saw, carpenter's square, steel tape, drill and bits, keyhole or coping saw

Tab-and-Slot Bench parts.

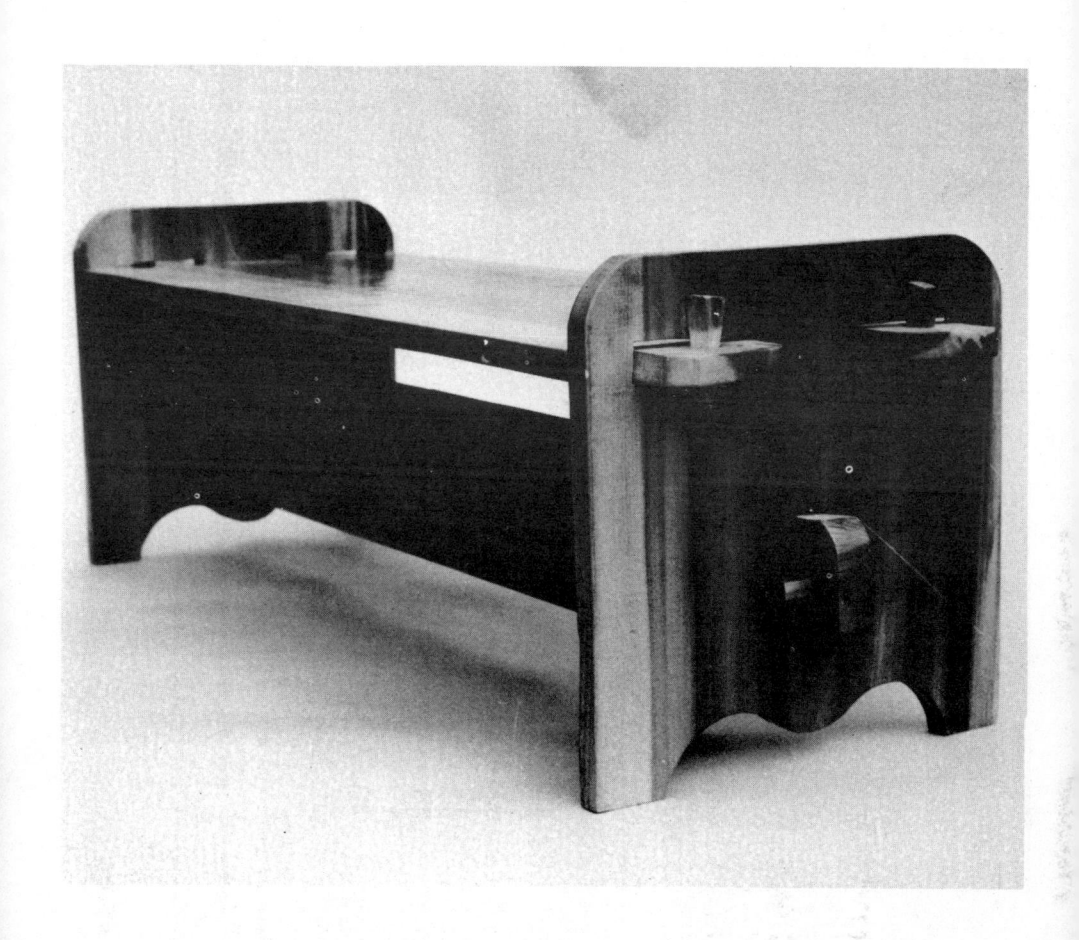

Tab-and-Slot Bench complete.

Building Instructions

Start with the legs. Cut two pieces of the same width 19 inches long from your 8-foot board. Set them aside. The remainder of the 8-foot piece is 58 inches long. This will be the bench seat. Cut the tabs as shown in Fig. 1. Round the corners on the tabs with your coping saw to give it a more professional look. Save the 2 x 4 pieces for the pegs.

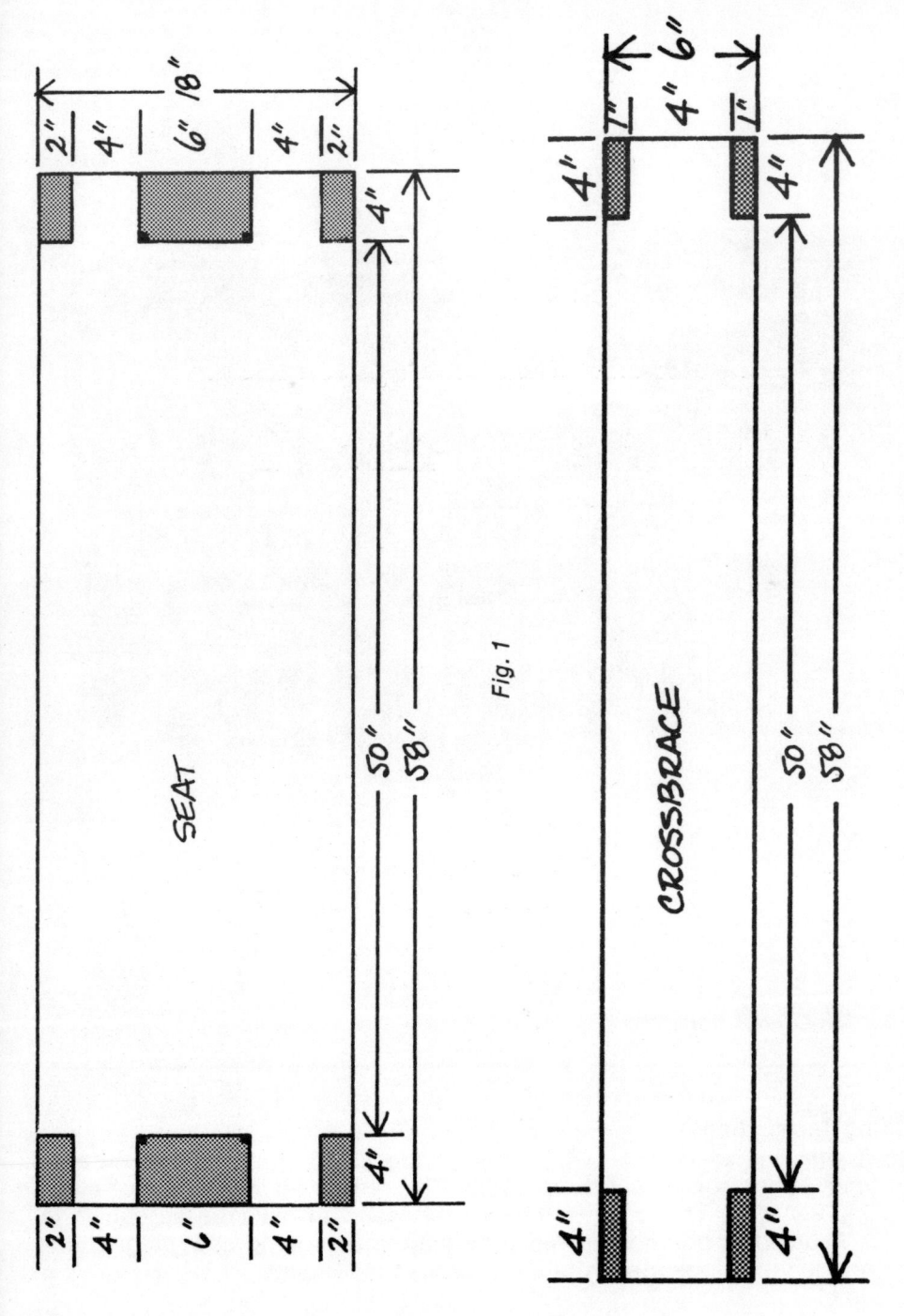

Fig. 1

Fig. 2

Take the 2 x 6 58-inch-long plank and cut it as shown in Fig. 2, cutting a 1-inch wide by 4-inch-long piece from each corner. Round the corners of the tabs with your coping saw. Save the 1 x 4 pieces for the pegs.

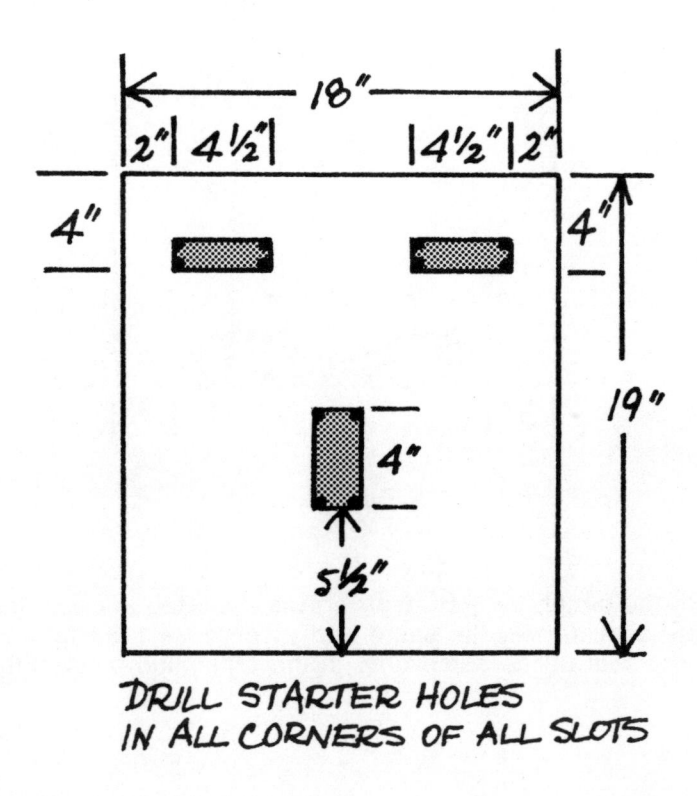

DRILL STARTER HOLES IN ALL CORNERS OF ALL SLOTS

Fig. 3

Now, cut the two 19-inch leg pieces as shown in Fig. 3. Cut both legs the same.

To add to the stability of your bench, and to enhance its appearance, cut out a design near the bottom with your coping saw. Mark the ends with a 6-inch protractor laid out as shown in Fig. 4.

Cut out the design and round the top corners, so the finished product resembles a smiling face. You can, of course, use a bowl, tin can, or any rounded instrument that will give you a similar outline.

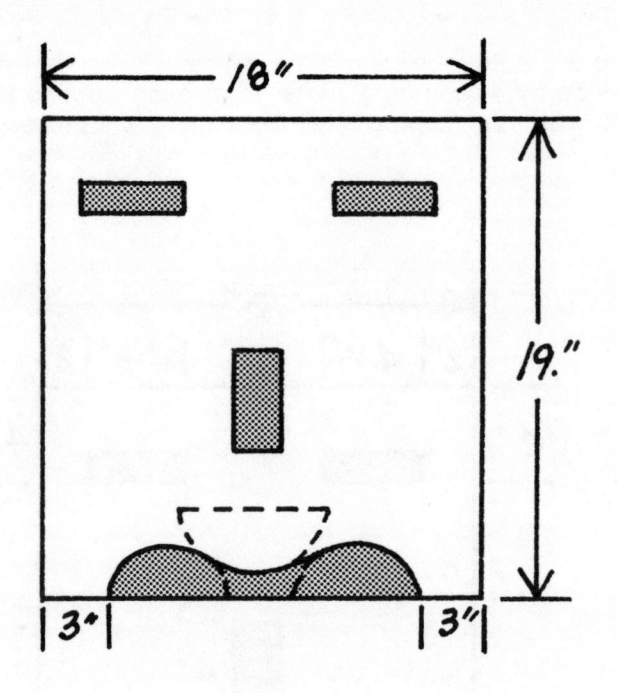

Fig. 4

Assemble the bench by first inserting the 2 x 6 tab in one leg piece, then inserting the seat tabs in the same end piece. Insert the tabs for both the 2 x 6 and the seat at the same time in the other end piece. Fit the pegs.

CHAPTER 16

TWO-FROM-ONE BENCH AND CHAIR

This set of plans is like getting two pounds of furniture from one pound of wood. Both the chair and the bench can be cut from one sheet of plywood. The bench plan is much like the bench on page 105, except that the brace is moved up to help support the seat.

The chair will need a 6-inch foam-covered cushion for the seat, and a 3-inch foam cushion for the back. You could use shredded foam for the seat cushion but a foam slab for the back will stand up better. If you can find some old sofa cushions of about the right size, so much the better. Cover the cushions with virtually any material, using the method described in Chapter 19 for the sofa.

You can style the sides of the chair like a deacon's bench, a church pew, or any other eye-pleasing shape.

	YOU WILL NEED
Wood	one 4' x 8' sheet of plywood or plateboard, good on both sides, or veneer
	pine or other wood scraps to make fourteen 4" long pegs
	veneer taping
Tools	saw, hole saw, drill and bits, carpenter's square, coping saw or keyhole saw

Fig. A

Two-From-One Chair.

Building Instructions

Lay out the sheet of plywood or plateboard as shown in Fig. 1. I find it best to mark everything out before cutting — even the tabs and slots, thus reducing the risk of a mistake, a bad cut, and a wasted piece of wood. As you can see from the drawings, there are many cuts and much room for error, so it is a good idea to mark everything first.

When making rounded corners, as for the side pieces of the chair and the end pieces of the bench, find a suitable round object. Push it to the corner to be rounded, then mark with a pencil along the edge. You can, of course, use a compass, but a coffee tin or a bowl work just as well.

Fig. B

Two-From-One Bench.

You can leave all the corners square, or cut the corners round after the pieces have been fitted together for the pegs. I like a rounded edge as it makes the furniture look softer.

The first cut is the one which will separate the bench ends and seat (the 18-inch wide pieces) from the rest. Cut these three pieces first, then cut the bench cross brace from the chair pieces. Now cut the slots and tabs for these four pieces. (See Chapter 15, Tab-and-Slot Bench for further instructions.)

Fit the pegs (see Chapter 5 on fitting pegs). You now have a finished bench to admire before starting the chair.

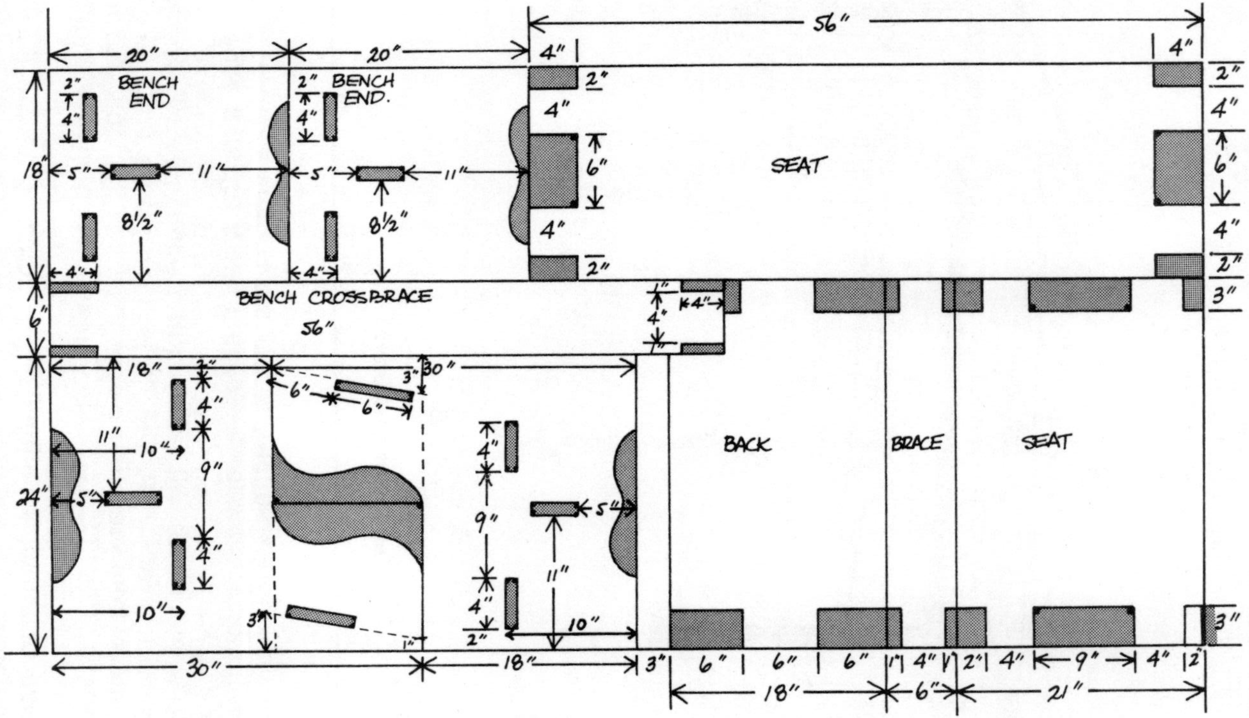

Fig. 1

Two Pieces of Furniture from One Piece of Plywood.

114

The chair has more pieces and more pegs, and takes longer to complete. Cut all the pieces for the chair. Round the corners. Cut out the tabs and slots, drilling starting holes at the slot corners as for the bench.

You will notice that one corner of the back has a piece missing. This will not weaken the chair, but when assembling it, make sure that it is put on the bottom and is thus hidden.

To assemble the chair, fit all the tabs into the slots on one side of the chair, then slide the other side onto the slots for the seat, the back, and the brace. This will probably take at least two pairs of hands. See Chapter 5 on fitting the pegs.

Two pieces of plywood set flat on the arms will make the chair more comfortable. Cut pieces 2 inches wide that will fit along the flat part of the arms. See Figure A. The length of the pieces will depend on how much rounding you did on your chair arms. Use three or four finishing nails and some glue to fasten the pieces in place.

If you like, you can glue veneer tape to the edges. It usually comes in 8-foot strips or rolls for about $1.25 each. Decide how many edges to cover—there is no need to cover all edges, only those which are exposed. Measure the edges (straight or curved) and purchase the required length

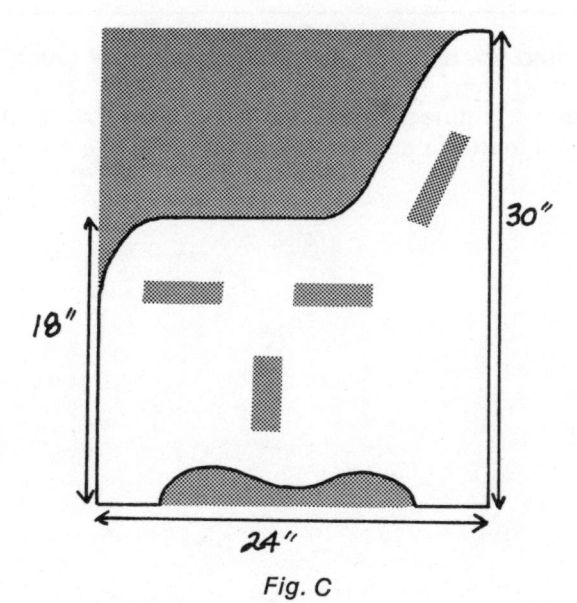

Fig. C

Suggestion for sculpting chair ends.

Fig. D   *Fig. E*

More ideas for sculpting chair ends.

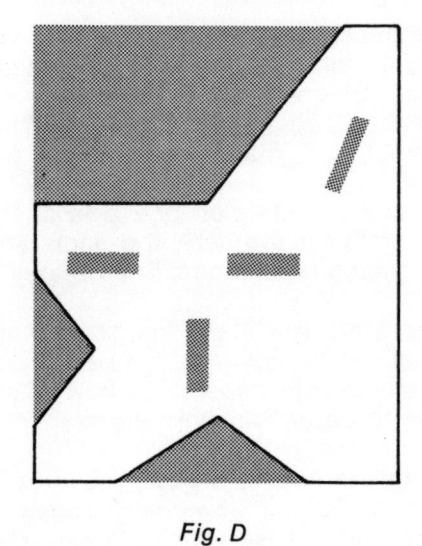

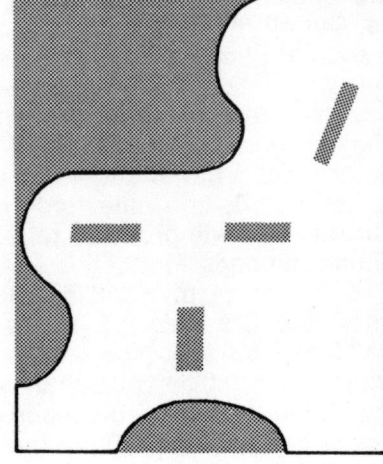

of tape. This can add up, as 8 feet does not cover very much. The tape may come in widths wider than ¾ inches. It can be trimmed with a sharp knife or razor blade after it is glued in place. Always glue the taping with contact cement — it eliminates the need to hold it in place while the glue is drying.

CHAPTER 17

TAKE-APART STORAGE CHEST

This storage box is very handy, especially if you move often, and do not have much storage space. Clothes, books, and any other clutter will find a home in it. It is also an ideal toy chest, as it is very strong.

If you want to take the box apart, simply pull out the rope hinge and remove the pegs. You can, of course, use the rope handles to carry it when fully assembled and filled. If you are going to use it as a permanent piece of furniture, get a thin foam pad, cover it, and put it on top of the box as a cushion. Do not be afraid to use the box, as it is strong, versatile, and durable.

I painted the outside of mine a deep blue, but left the rope and pegs their natural color.

The box is 48 inches long, 16 inches wide, 14 inches deep. The exterior is 54 x 24 x 20.

YOU WILL NEED	
Wood	one 4' x 8' plywood or plateboard sheet
Rope	¼" or ⅜" 12' long (plastic, manilla, nylon)
Tools	saw, square, tape measure, keyhole saw, drill and bit

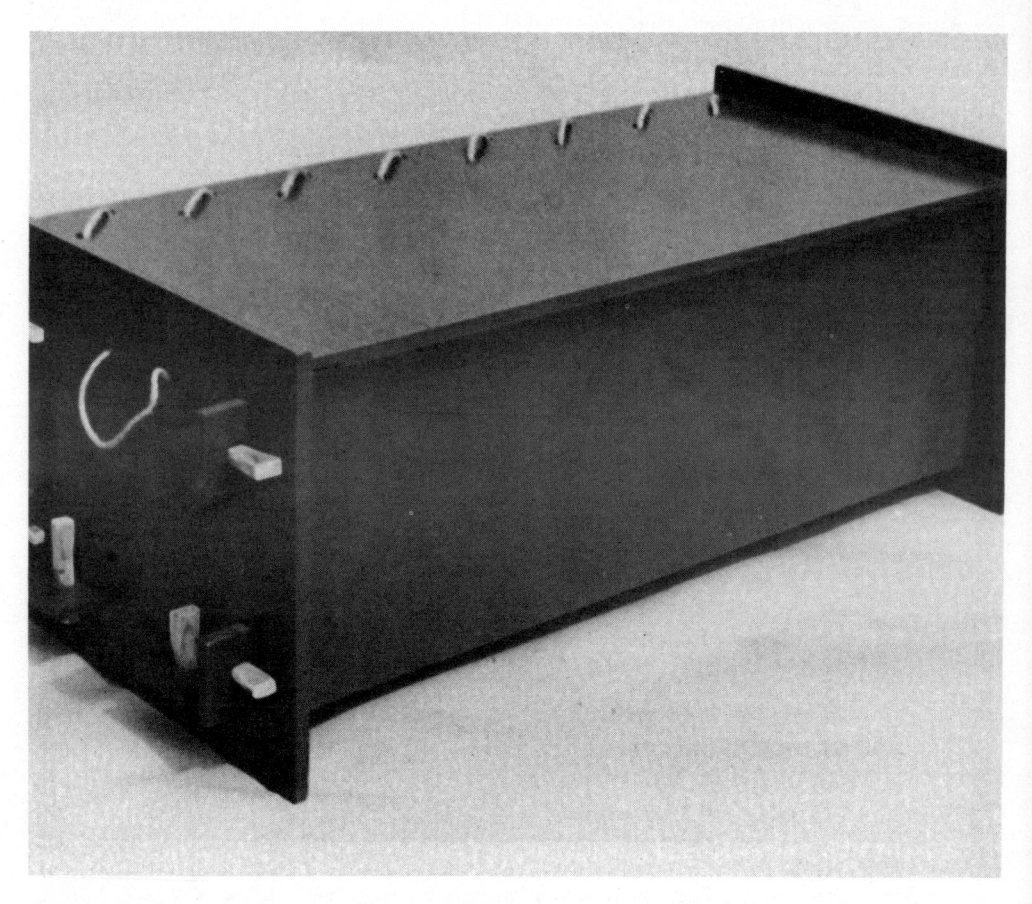

Storage Chest/Toy Box/Bench complete with lid closed.

Building Instructions

Mark the sheet and cut it as shown in Fig. 1. You will notice that the sides and bottom are identical in every respect. These 54 x 16-inch pieces are interchangeable, so mark and cut all tabs exactly the same. The end pieces are also interchangeable, so mark and cut the slots identically. The 22 x 48 piece is the top. Trim about ¾ inches off the length (to 47¼ inches). This will give it a bit of extra room to hinge.

Cut out all the tabs and slots as shown in Fig. 1. The slots will be about 1 inch wide and about 4¼ inches long, which will allow extra room for fitting.

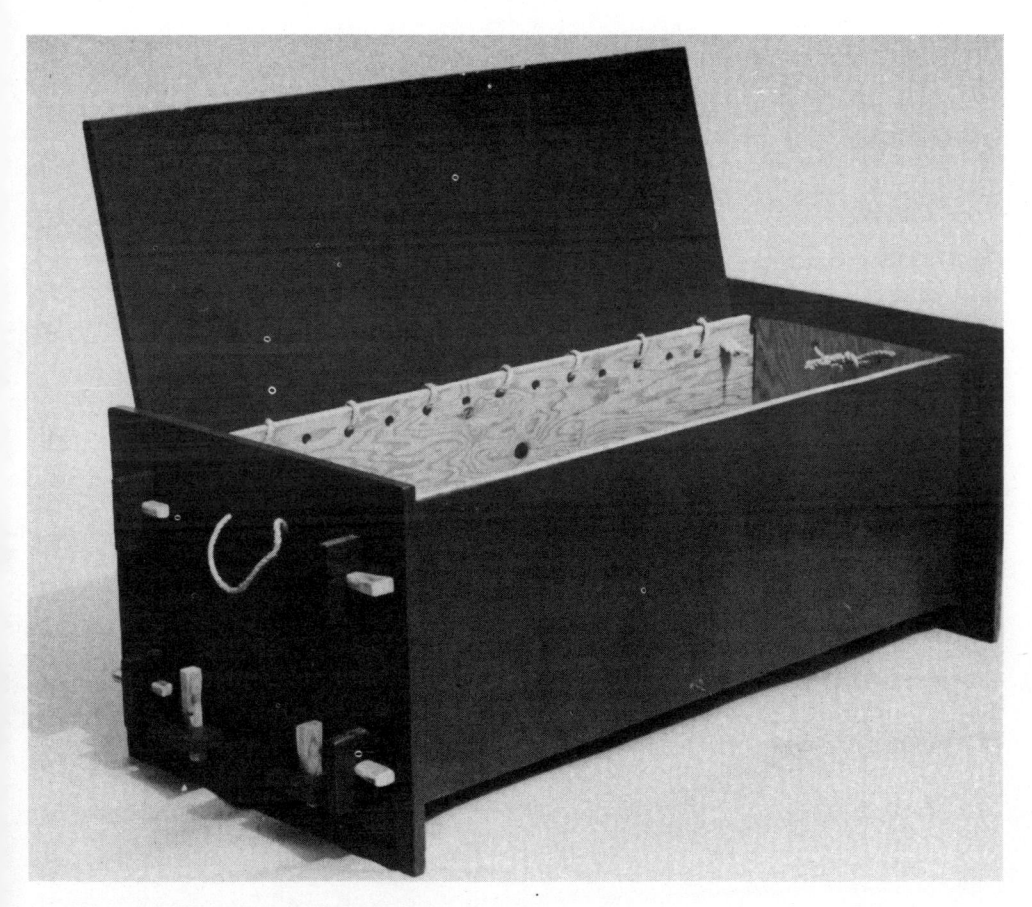

Storage Chest/Toy Box/Bench complete with lid open.

Assemble the box, inserting the bottom and the sides into the slots on one end piece, then sliding the other end on. If using plywood, the good side will be on the outside. See Chapter 5 on fitting pegs.

When the pegs have been fitted, drill the holes for the rope. Begin by putting the top on the box. The top should have an overhang of about 2¼ inches over the front and back edges. Mark a line along the underside of the back edge of the lid where it overhangs the side piece. (See Figs. 2 and 4.)

Draw two lines parallel to the first line, about 1½ inches on either side of it. Along the two outer lines you will drill your holes. Start marking on

119

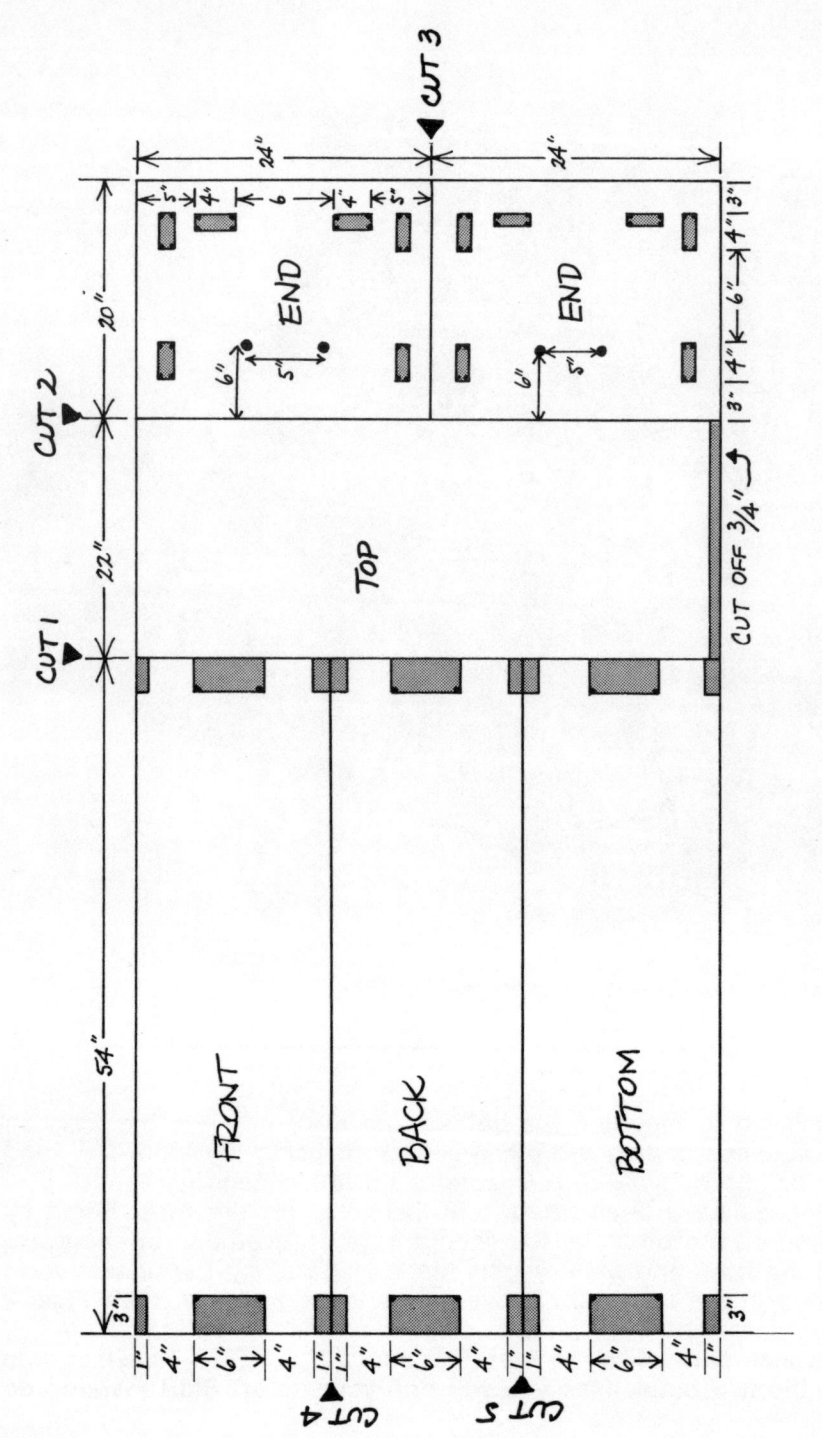

Fig. 1

the line nearest the lid edge from the left side. Mark a crosshatch at 3 inches from this end, then one every 6 inches. On the other line (the one closer to the front of the lid), mark the first crosshatch 6 inches from the end, then every 6 inches. (Fig. 2.)

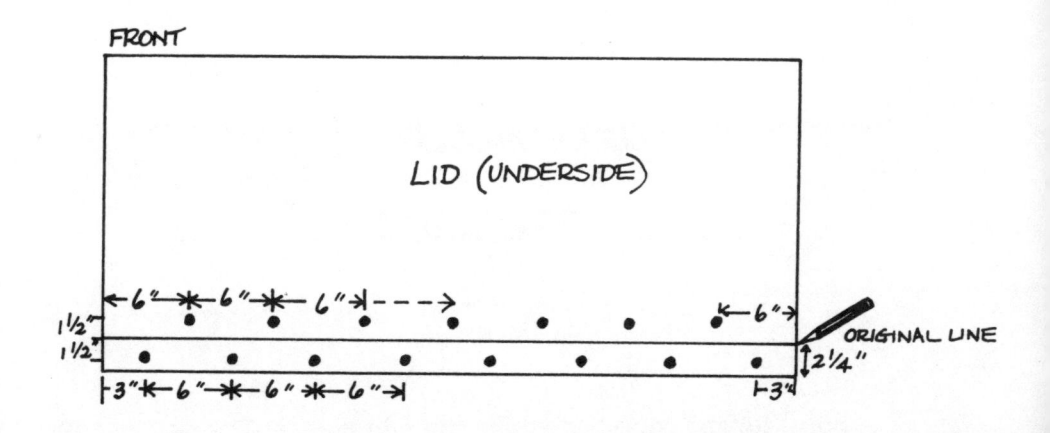

Fig. 2

With the lid off, mark a line on the box about 1½ inches down from the upper edge of the back side piece. Mark the crosshatches along this line from the left side at 2 inches from the end, then every 6 inches. (Fig. 3.)

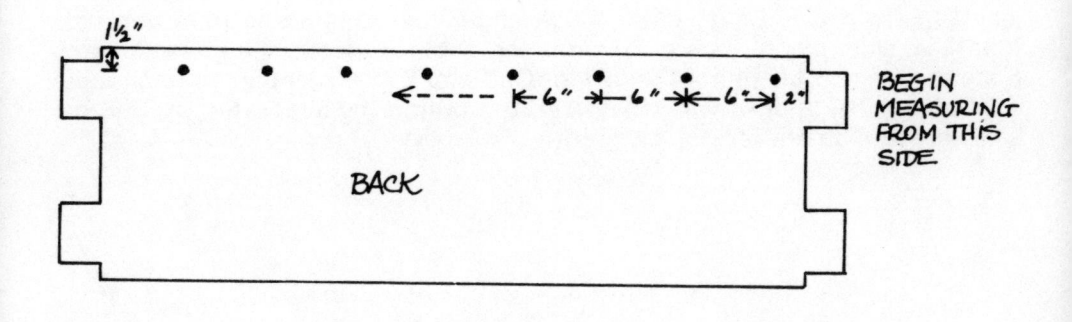

Fig. 3

121

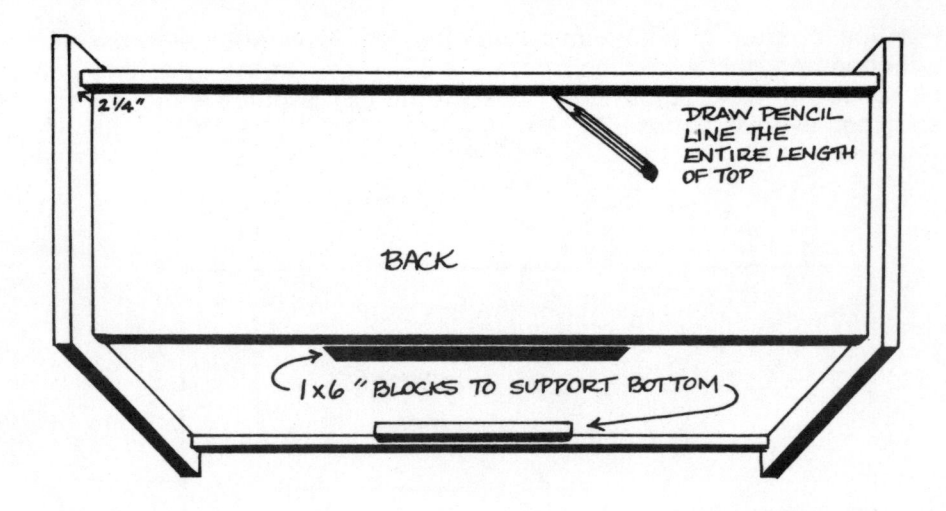

Fig. 4

Mark the holes for the rope handles in the end pieces. The holes should be about 5 inches apart, about 3 inches below the level of the lid, and centered on the end piece. Drill the holes ⅛ of an inch larger than the rope — I used ¼-inch rope and drilled ⅜-inch holes. Clean away the splinters from around the holes. For the hinge lace the rope through the holes. Leave some slack so the lid can move easily. Loop the rope for the handles through the holes and tie it together with a square knot. Simply tie a knot in each end of the hinge rope to keep it in place.

When everything fits together well, remove the ropes (so as not to get paint or varnish on them), and apply the finish of your choice.

Note: If you load the box really full with very heavy things, the bottom may sag. To prevent sag, put a block under the bottom and glue and nail it to the side piece. There is room for a block about 1-inch wide and 6 inches long to fit, without showing. One block in the center of each side will suffice. The blocks will strengthen the bottom by supporting it, but the box will still dismantle. (Fig. 4.)

CHAPTER 18

CAPTAIN'S CHAIR

This chair is a little more complicated than the Indian chair of Chapter 8, but as four-legged chairs go, it is not at all difficult. You should be able to make it for about $10.00. I cut the cost of mine by using leftover materials for the back and seat.

	YOU WILL NEED
Wood	pine, cedar, spruce, fir, any soft wood
	1" x 3" (actually 2½" wide) two 32" pieces
	two 22½" pieces
	two 20" pieces
	three 23" pieces
	one 21½" piece
	1" x 8" two 20" pieces
Cloth	one 8" x 30" length
	one 10" x 48" length
	one 18" x 36" length
Hardware	twelve ¼" x 2" carriage bolts with twelve flat washers
	One gross ½" carpet tacks
	Sixteen No. 8 1½" flat-head wood screws
Tools	saw, carpenter's square, drill and bits, screwdriver, hammer, wrench or pliers, file, hacksaw

Captain's Chair complete.

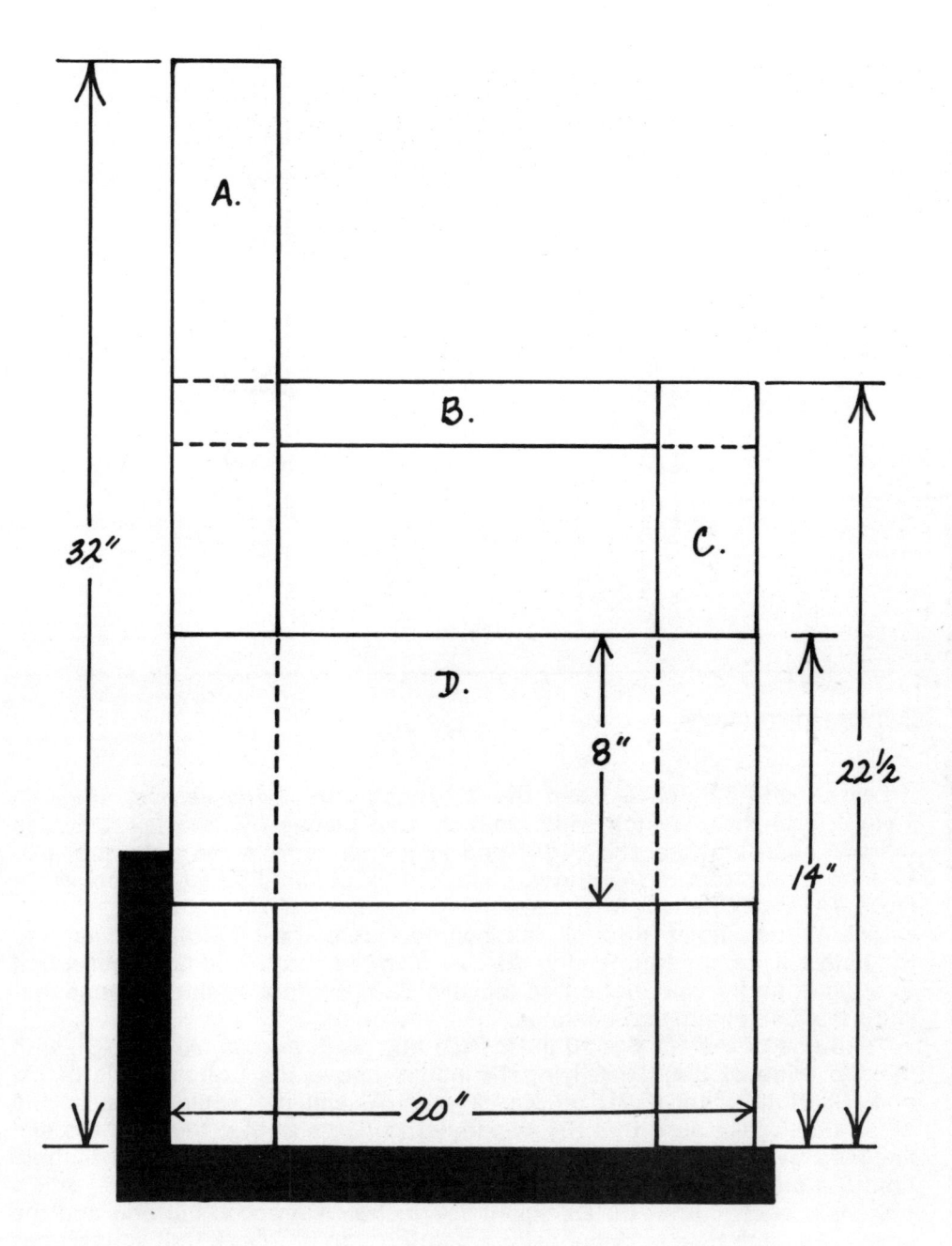

Fig. 1

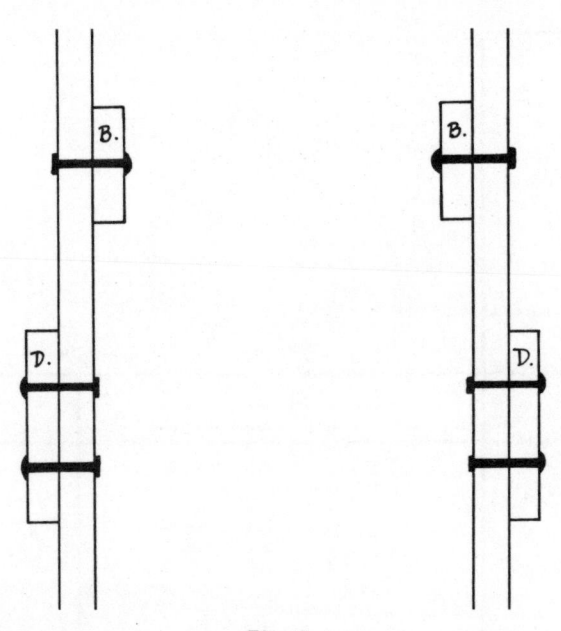

Fig. 2

Building Instructions

Lay out the 32-inch (A) and the 22½-inch (C) pieces parallel. (Fig. 1.) Take one of the 2½-inch wide, 20-inch long pieces (B) and lay it across the two boards at the end of (C) and 22½ inches from the bottom of (A). Line up the bottom of (A) and (C) with the carpenter's square as shown in Fig. 1. (A) and (C) are now parallel.

Drill ¼-inch holes through the boards where they intersect, centering the hole 1¼ inches from each edge. As soon as you drill a hole, put a bolt through it, and screw the nut on loosely. Turn over these three pieces that you have just joined, and continue.

Take one of the 1 x 8 x 20 pieces (D) and lay it across (A) and (C), with the top edge of the 1 x 8 lying 14 inches above the bottom ends of (A) and (C). Notice that (B) is on one side of (A) and (C), while (D) is on the other side. Make sure that (D) is parallel to (B), and that the legs are still lined up evenly. Check with the square. You may need a friend to help hold the pieces. When everything is parallel and even on the ends, drill a hole near each corner of (D), about 1¼ inches from both the end and the edges. As each hole is drilled, slip a bolt through it. Check that your pieces are still in their proper places before drilling the next hole. When all four

FLOOR

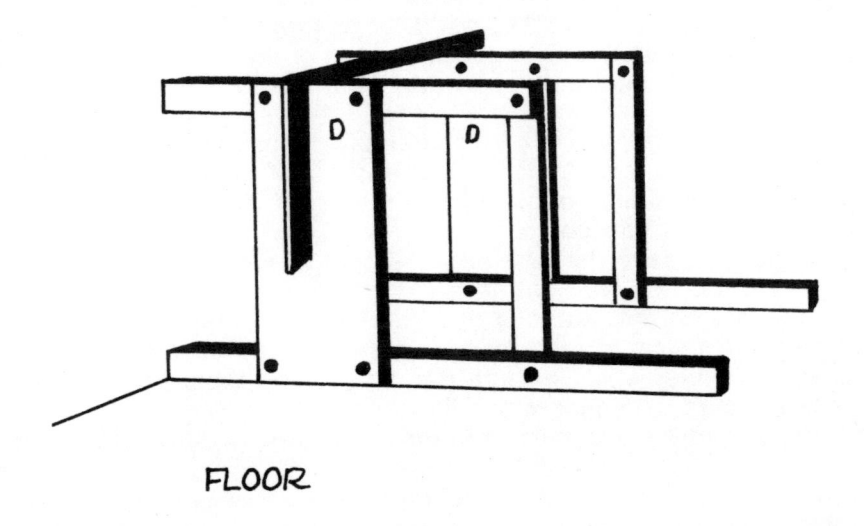

Fig. 3

holes have been drilled, put the nuts and washers on the bolts, but leave them loose. Set aside.

You now have half a chair. Next, construct the other half. Remember, however, that the two halves are not identical — the arms (B) of the second half should be on the inside of the uprights, and the reinforcing piece (D) should be on the outside of the uprights. (Fig. 2.)

Thus you have a right and a left side. Follow the procedure as outlined for the first side, but make sure that the two sides are as shown in Fig. 2.

When both halves have been built, attach the crosspieces. There are four. Start by lying your chair on its back with the legs against a wall, as shown in Fig. 3. Or, lean it against anything solid that will keep the legs even.

While someone helps you hold the legs against a wall, check with the carpenter's square to ensure that the two chair halves are perpendicular to the floor and the wall, thus ensuring that the pieces are absolutely parallel. Take one of the 23-inch pieces and lay it across the ends of piece (D) (Fig. 3), with the top of this crosspiece even with the top of the 1 x 8 (D).

Drill the four screw pilot holes through the crosspiece and into the uprights. Then make the countersink and drill shank holes (see page 44). Attach this board with four screws.

Turn the chair over and attach the back crosspiece in the same manner, with four screws, and even with the top of the 1 x 8.

Next, the crosspiece near the top of the uprights. This is the piece 21½ inches long. Line it up 3 inches below the top of the uprights with the ends flush, drill pilot holes for the screws, and attach this piece with four screws.

You now have one piece of wood left. It goes underneath the 1 x 8 pieces, connecting them. Attach it just in front of the 32-inch long upright pieces with the remaining four screws.

The chair frame is now complete.

Check that you have the bolt heads shown in Fig. 2. They are the best, as they are out of the way and less likely to snag clothes. Check that the flat washers are on the nut ends of all the bolts. Tighten the bolts until the heads begin to pull into the wood. Cut the threads off the bolts with the hacksaw where they stick through the nut, cutting them off flush with the nut. Smooth the rough edges with a file.

At this point round some corners on the boards to make the chair look less boxy.

A couple of tips: If your chair wobbles because of slightly uneven legs, or slightly misplaced screws or bolts, here is how to correct it: Put a piece of board across the 1 x 8 pieces and have someone sit on it. Loosen all the bolts until there is no tension on them. Then, while the person is sitting in the chair, tighten them. This will correct **minor** imperfections. If it does not correct your problem, you will have to start trimming wood.

If the chair is going to be rocked on its back legs, glue the joints. I have not had to do this, but it might be necessary in some cases.

To glue the joints, remove the nuts and flat washers from the bolts and slide the boards slightly apart. Apply some glue between the boards and rebolt each piece before taking the next joint apart.

If you are going to put a finish on, do it now, before upholstering.

Hanging the Cloth

Any good, heavy fabric will do. Heavy canvas and drapery material, hopsack, leather, plastic upholstery material, all work well. For my chair, I used some leftovers from the sofa covering.

The dimensions of the cloth allow a ½-inch overlap on the edges for a seam. Cut the cloth into:

> one 8 x 30 piece for the back
> one 10 x 48 piece for the seat crosspiece
> one 18 x 36 piece for the seat.

If you are using material that will fray, sew an edge seam now.

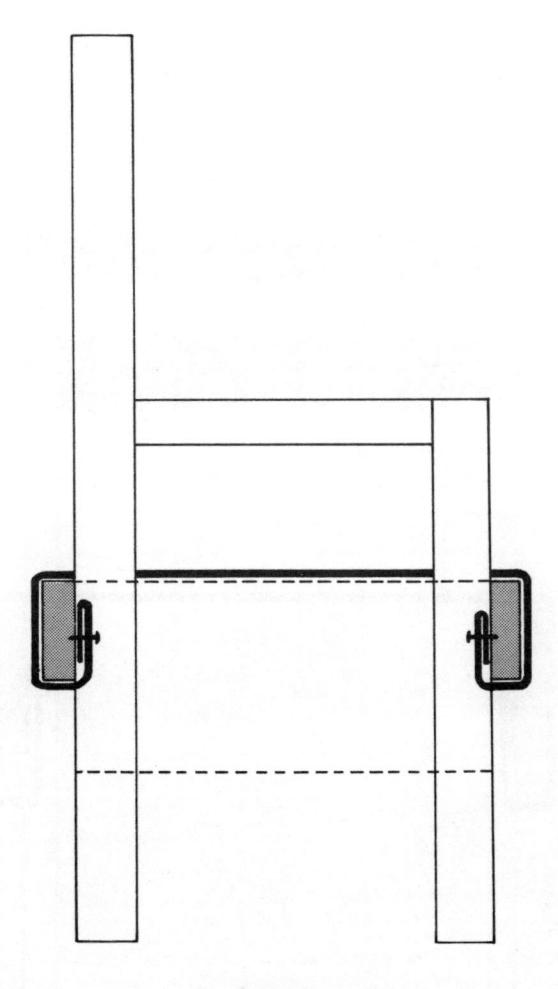

Fig. 4

Begin by tacking the seat piece (18 x 36) on the inside of the front crosspiece, with the length of cloth facing towards the floor. Fold down about 1 inch of the width so you are tacking on a double layer of cloth. Put in a tack approximately every inch along the width of the material. (Fig. 4.)

When the front end has been tacked on, pull it over the back crosspiece. Pull it really tight, fold the excess cloth under, and tack to the inside of the crosspiece.

Next, take the 10 x 48 piece for the seat crosspiece. Fold under about 1 inch and tack to the inside of the 1 x 8 with the material trailing downward towards the floor. (Fig. 5.)

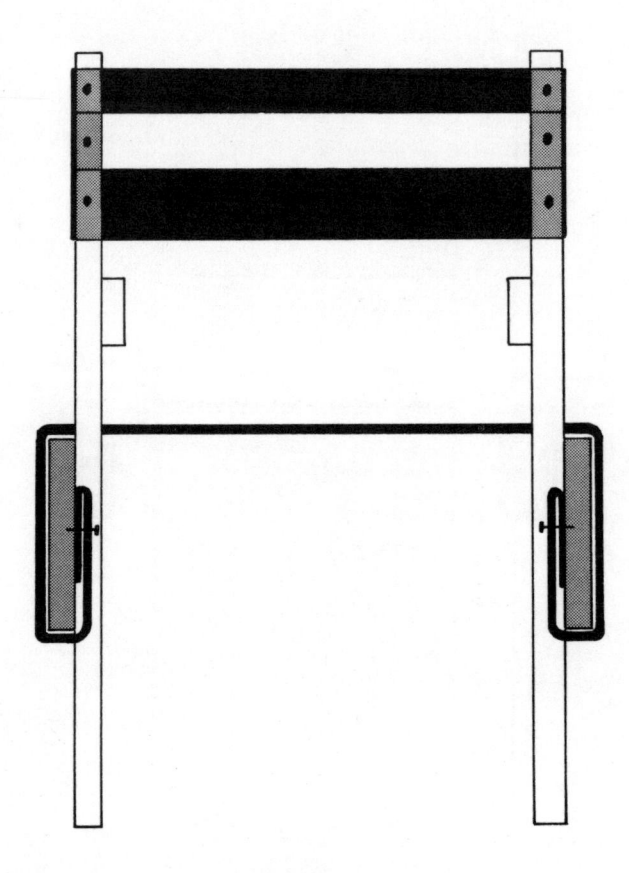

Fig. 5

When one end has been tacked on, pull the cloth around the outside of the 1 x 8, under the seat material, on the outside of the opposite 1 x 8 and tack to the inside of it. Stretch this tight, fold the excess cloth under, and insert one tack every inch as before.

The remaining back piece is tacked on to the uprights at the very top. Fold under 1 inch of the cloth and tack every inch. The crosspiece will be

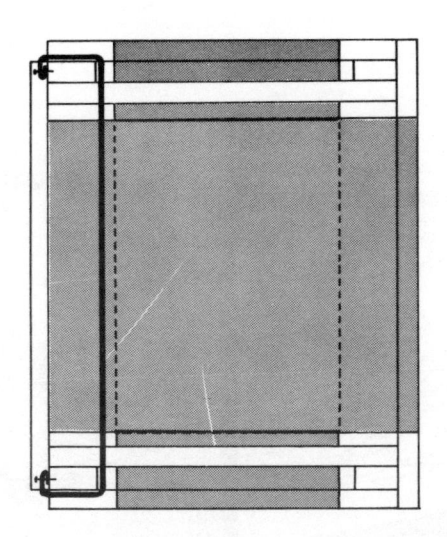

Fig. 6

in the way, but just tack the cloth up and over it. You should not have any problem with the few tacks on the crosspiece, or the few above and below it. (Fig. 6.) Stretch the cloth tight across the front of the uprights and tack it the same way on the opposite upright.

'Ave a seat, Cap'n!

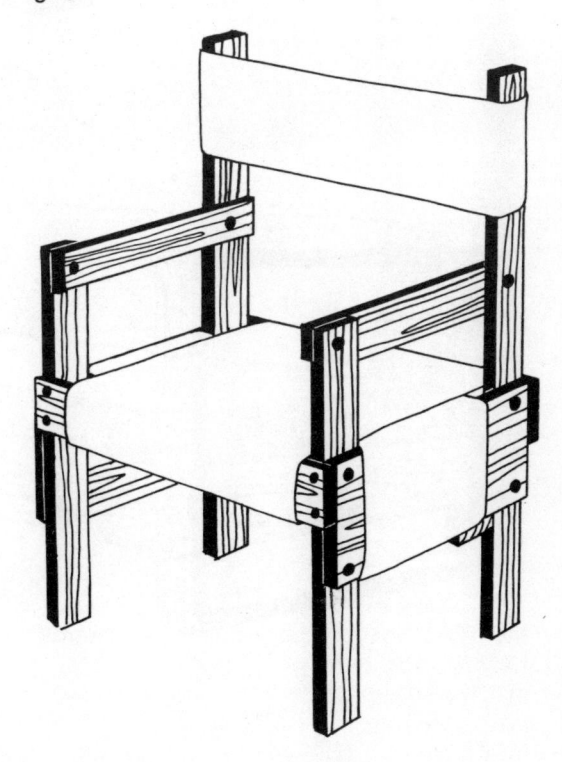

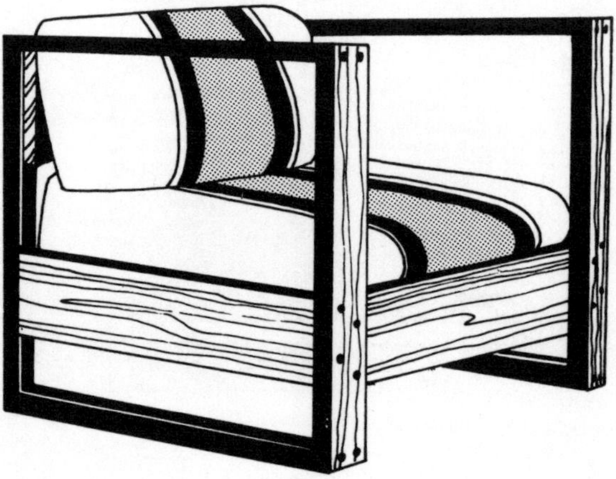

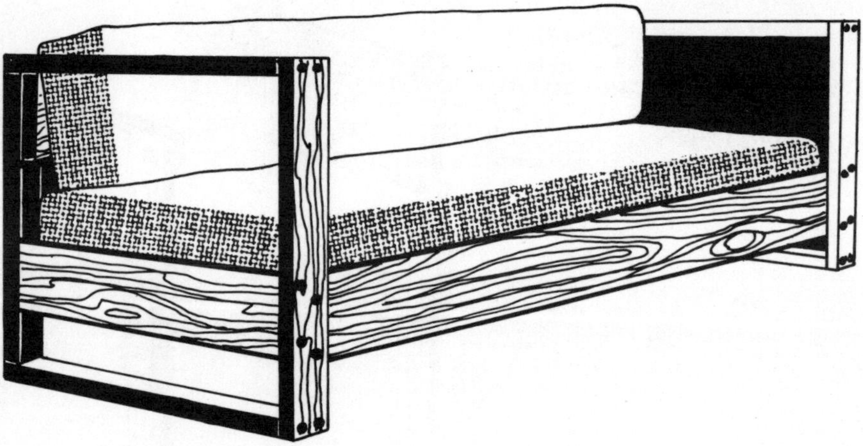

CHAPTER 19

ADJUSTABLE SOFA AND MATCHING CHAIRS

Although easy to build, this sofa will take more time than the other pieces. It will cost between $75.00 and $80.00. The design is simple, but attractive. The back cushion of the sofa lifts off to convert into a temporary bed for an overnight guest.

The sofa can be made any length, simply by shortening or lengthening the three 2 x 8s which connect the end pieces, and adjusting the length of the foam and cloth. You can also make matching chairs by constructing the end pieces in the same manner as the sofa, by making the 2 x 8s which connect the end pieces about 28 inches long, or, whatever chair width suits you.

	YOU WILL NEED
Wood	four 2" x 4"s 28" long
	four 2" x 4" 32" long
	two 2" x 8"s 32" long
	two 2" x 8"s 73" long
	one 2" x 8" 76½" long
	two 2" x 2"s 72" long
	enough 1" boards or ¾" plywood to cover a surface 28" wide x 71" long
Cloth	six yards of 45" width (or a minimum of 84" wide 106" long) of any upholstery cloth or other material heavy enough to use as a cover.
Foam	one 6" deep foam pad 40" x 72"
	(or two 3" deep foam pads)
Hardware	fourteen No. 10 3" flat-headed wood screws
	thirty-two ¼" 3" lag bolts with flat washers
	two 3" corner braces with four screws each
Tools	saw, square, steel tape, drill and bits, socket wrench (to fit lag bolts)

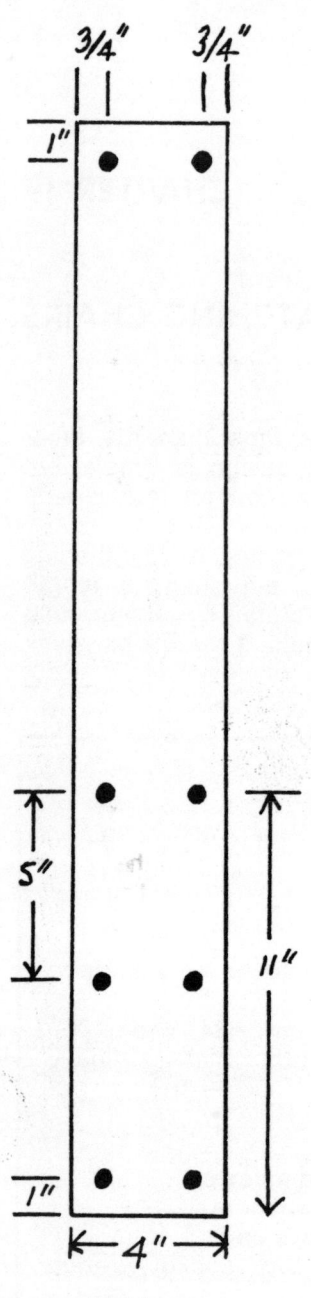

Fig. 1

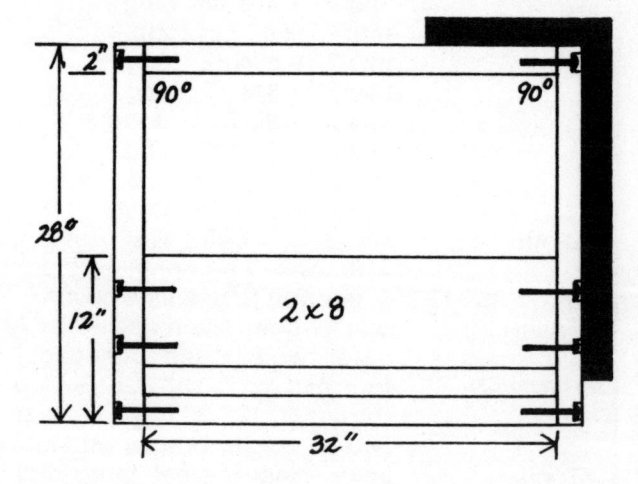

Fig. 2

134

Building Instructions

Begin by cutting the 28 and the 32-inch 2 x 4s and 2 x 8s. Use your square. Make sure all cuts are straight.

Lay out all four 28-inch 2 x 4s as shown in Fig. 1. Drill a ¾-inch hole about half an inch deep at each crosshatch, as indicated in Fig. 1. These holes are to countersink the lag bolts which will hold the frame together. (Fig. 1.)

Take two of the 28-inch 2 x 4s and two of the 32-inch 2 x 4s and one 2 x 8 32 inches long, and lay them out as shown in Fig. 2. The 2 x 4s are on edge, the 2 x 8 is flat. The 2 x 8 should fit between the 2 x 4s; if it is a bit long, trim it now. Let the 2 x 8 lie flush with either edge of the 2 x 4s. (Fig. 2.)

Put a 5/32-inch bit into your drill. Hold the square next to your pieces, as shown in Fig. 2. This is to ensure that the corners are square. Drill a 5/32-inch hole through the center of the ¾-inch hole as deep as you can through the first 2 x 4 and into the next. This is the pilot hole for the lag bolts. Enlarge the 5/32-inch hole through only the **first** 2 x 4 to ¼ of an inch so that your lag bolt will slip through this hole and into its pilot hole. Take a lag bolt, put a flat washer on it, and turn it into the hole until it is fairly tight.

Now is the time when you find out whether or not you have cut the 2 x 4s straight. If the lag bolt pulls the wood crooked, you may have to insert a wood chip for filler between the 2 x 4s to keep everything straight. Proceed as outlined above through all four corners.

When you have drilled the four corners, move the 2 x 8 so that its upper edge is 12 inches from the bottom of the 2 x 4 rectangle you have just made, and so that it corresponds with two of the remaining countersink holes. (Fig. 2.) Leave your rectangle of 2 x 4s lying flat, so that the lower flat edge of the 2 x 8 is flush with the edges of the 2 x 4s. When the 2 x 8 is in position, drill the 5/32-inch hole, the ¼-inch hole, and insert the lag bolt, as you did previously. You have now completed one end of the sofa. Make the other exactly the same.

Cut your remaining 2 x 8s to the length that you want your sofa. Have someone hold the 2 x 4 rectangles upright, so that the 2 x 8s that are bolted to the inside of the rectangles are on the outer edge, and the top edge of the 2 x 8 is 12 inches off the floor. Hold one 2 x 8 (73 inches long) up so its top edge is also 12 inches from the floor, and flush with the top of the neighboring 2 x 8, yet against both that 2 x 8 and the 2 x 4.

Both ends of the 2 x 8 must be 12 inches off the floor. You will see how the two remaining countersunk holes match this plank. Now drill the 5/32-inch hole, the ¼-inch hole, and insert the lag bolts. Drill the other end of that plank, then the other 2 x 8 (73 inches long) opposite it in the same manner.

The remaining 2 x 8 (76½ inches long) is for the back support. It should fit into the top corner at the back of the sofa. (At this point, you will have to choose which is the front and which the back.)

Drill the holes to hold this piece. Drill two pilot holes from the back of the 2 x 4 and into the 2 x 8. Enlarge the pilot hole through the 2 x 4 only, with a ¼-inch drill for the lag bolt to slip through. You will use two bolts at each end of the 2 x 8.

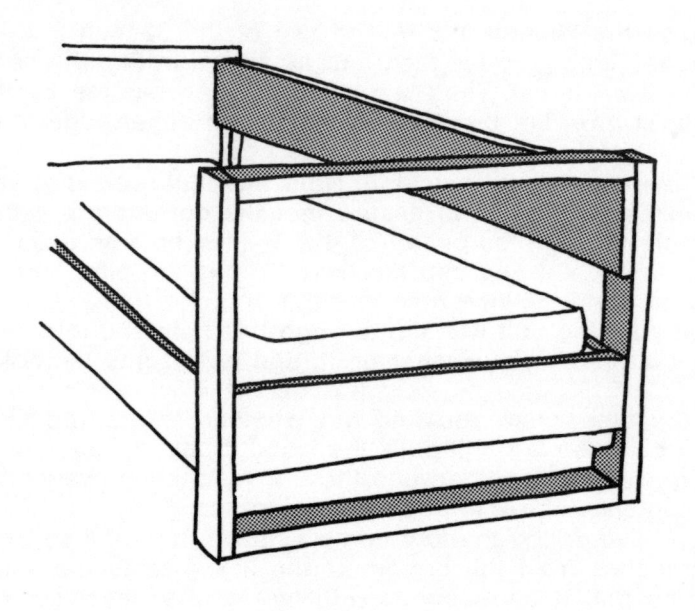

Fig. 3

The completed frame should look like that in Fig. 3.

Place the 3-inch angle braces in the front upper corners of the 2 x 4 rectangles — one per corner. Center them on the 2 x 4s and attach them with four screws each. (Fig. 4.)

The 2 x 2 72-inch pieces fit along the inside of the 73-inch long 2 x 8s. These are to hold the boards which the foam seat will rest on. They should be about 2 inches above the bottom edge of the 2 x 8, on the inside. Secure them with the 3-inch screws. Space the screws 12 inches apart along the 2 x 2. Drill a pilot hole for the screws and then the screw-shank holes. Attach the 2 x 2s. (Fig. 5.)

When both the 2 x 2s are in place, you will need the boards for the foam to rest on. I used old scrap boards of various widths, cut 28 inches long.

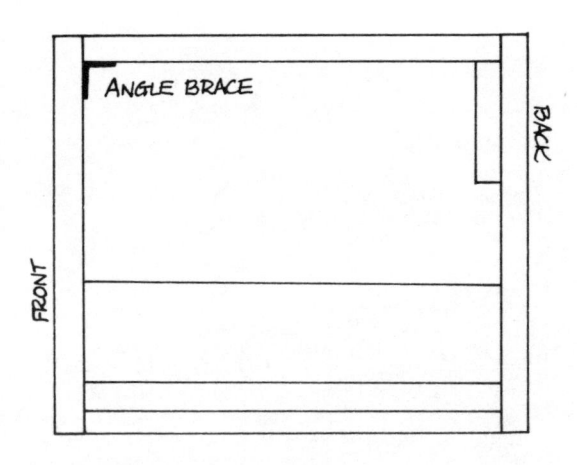

Fig. 4

The width does not matter, but the general rule is the wider the better. You can also use a piece of ¾-inch plywood 28 x 72 instead of the boards. These boards (or plywood) will lie on the 2 x 2s, spanning the gap, lying perpendicular to the 2 x 2s. They do not need to be fastened.

Your frame is complete, ready for finishing. A tip for the finishing touches: sometimes one 2 x 4 is just a little wider than another. Check the corners of your 2 x 4 rectangles. If one side of a 2 x 4 sticks out from (is wider than) another, use your plane and shave it down near the end so everything is perfectly flush.

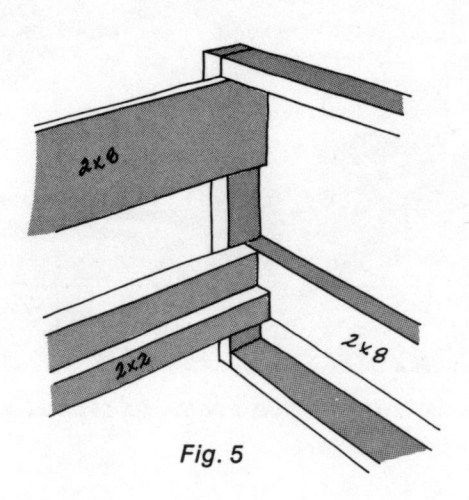

Fig. 5

Sofa frame complete. Sofa frame with boards to support seat cushion.

The finished sofa.

Upholstering

You will note that I specify one foam pad, when you actually need two. The seat cushion is 26 inches wide, the back is 14 inches wide. You can get foam custom-cut to these widths, but if this is too expensive, or if this service is not available, you can easily cut it yourself. Any long-bladed sharp knife will do. I cut mine with a serrated-edge bread knife.

Mark the line with a pencil or magic marker, using a long board for a straight edge. Do not try to saw the knife through the whole thickness at once, but make slashes about 2 inches deep, pull the slit open, make another slash, and so forth, working along the length of the foam. Do not worry if you have a slightly ragged cut; it will not show.

Sew your cloth together until you have a continuous width about 12 inches or more longer than the foam, or a minimum of about 84 inches. Cut the cloth to a 29½-inch length for the back, and 66½ inches for the seat. Sew these pieces into a tube, using a ½-inch overlap for the seam. (Fig. 6.)

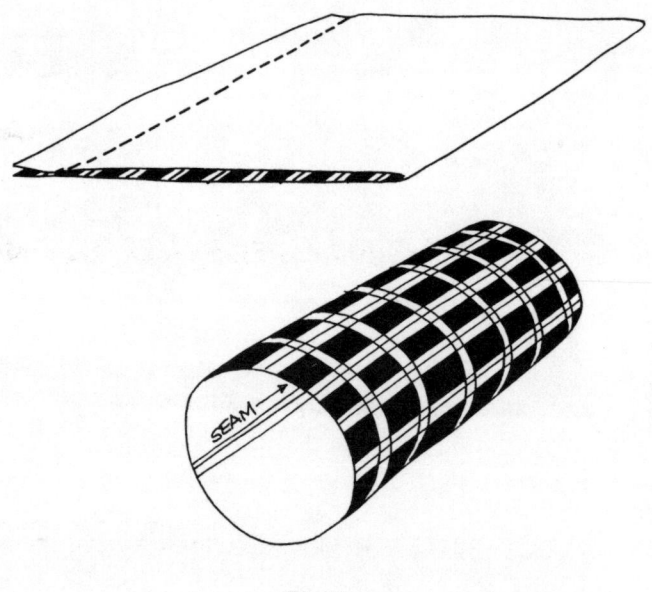

Fig. 6

These tubes of cloth should slide snugly over the foam pads. Start the seam along one edge of the cushion. It will be less noticeable there. Pull the cloth over the foam, a few inches at a time, until the tube completely covers the foam. It does not matter which side up you leave your cushions. This is great for hiding those inevitable stains and cigarette burns; you just flip it over. You can also pull the cloth off again to wash it. Sew the ends together, folding and tucking them neatly.

CHAPTER 20

TRADITIONAL PEDESTAL DINING TABLE

The pedestal table is a very fine piece of furniture, really beautiful in its rugged simplicity. Traditionally the pedestal table was round or oval. These shapes are difficult for the amateur carpenter, with only a few hand tools, to master. The hexagon shape used here is easier, as all cuts are straight and there are no difficult joints. It is really quite simple to build.

I made mine of oak planks. I salvaged some 18 x 2 pieces of thick oak which had been intended for some sea-wall planking. The planks were not furniture-grade, but average construction-grade wood. They had knots and checks, but the finished product is spectacular.

You can use soft wood, but hardwood wears better. Soft wood dents with heavy use. Pine, fir, or spruce are easy to get and will work fine, but if hardwood is available at a reasonable price, use it.

Finish by applying numerous coats of urethane. I put six coats on mine. It makes the surface very hard, resisting scratches and general abuse.

When I built my table, the planks were not dry enough. Two cracks about half an inch wide appeared. It still looked all right, but eventually I pushed the two pieces together by removing the screws from the backing pieces. Remember, it is easier to make sure your wood is dry in the first place!

The wood for the tabletop can be bought in any width, but the wider the planks the better. If you buy enough wood to cover the 52 x 62 area, you will have enough, with some left over. But remember, lumber is never the width that it is advertised. A 12-inch wide plank is usually only 11¼ inches wide. This does differ from region to region, so be prepared for some calculations at the lumberyard. Also, the wood might shrink a bit. Get the wood as close to the right dimensions as possible, then make minor adjustments later.

Hexagon Table complete.

You can, of course, also scale down the size of the table.

The legs of the pedestal actually span about 40 inches. Thus you can make the table considerably smaller by scaling down the hexagon top, but still using the same dimensions for the pedestal.

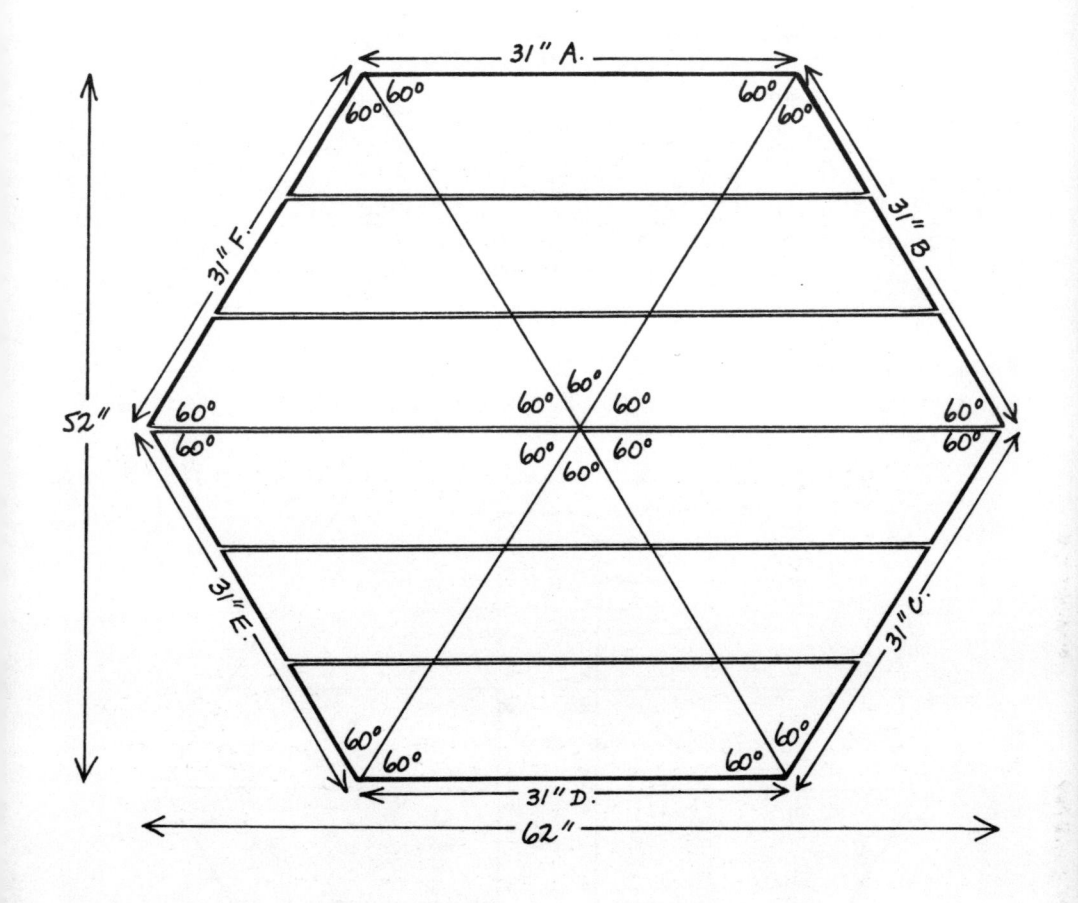

Fig. 1

When scaling down, remember that all angles are 60 degrees. The minimum size for this table is about 24 inches per side, about the width of one table setting. This will accommodate six people. (Fig. 1.)

Make a full-size pattern of the top from newspapers before you cut any wood. Tape some pages together and measure the whole thing out, using a felt-tip marker. (Fig. 1.)

	YOU WILL NEED
Wood	all 2" thick
	top — 52" x 62" (see above)
	one 2" x 8" 12' long
	one 2" x 4" 10' long
	two 1½" x 1½" (or 2" x 2") 8' long
Hardware	five dozen No. 10 3" screws
	four 3" angle braces with four screws each

Building Instructions

When your wood has dried and is ready to use, and your pattern for the top has been made, you can begin.

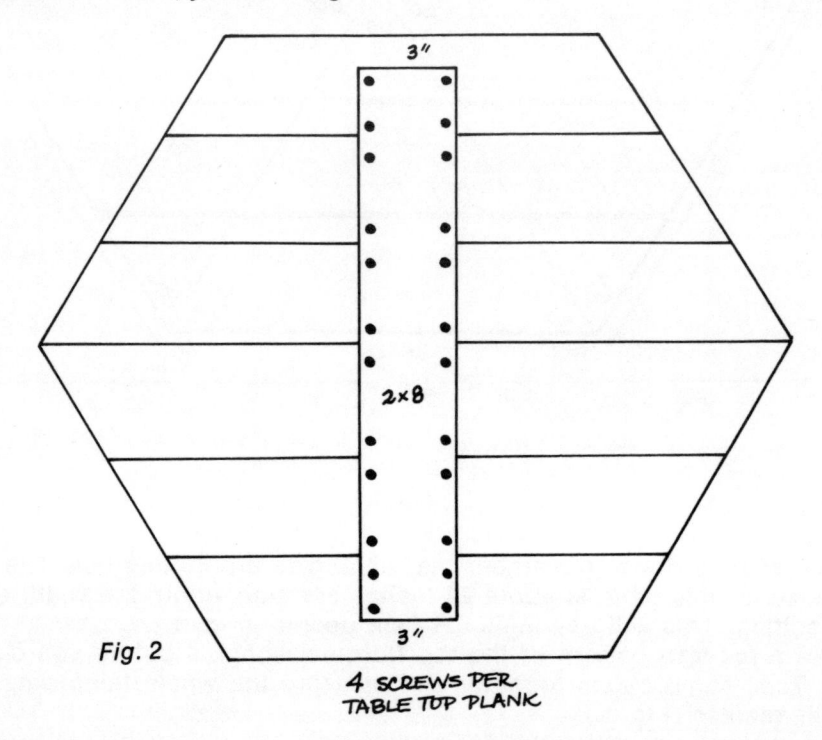

Fig. 2

4 SCREWS PER TABLE TOP PLANK

Lay the planks for the top tightly beside each other. If the planks do not lie together snugly, you may have to change them around, switching them end for end, or flipping them over. And you may have to plane a bit off some edges. (see Chapter 4 on joining narrow planks). At the same time, select which side of the planks is best suited for the top.

When you are satisfied with how the planks look, lay your pattern over them. Mark the planks and then cut them into the right lengths and angles.

Now reassemble the tabletop, with the right side facing down.

Measure across the hexagon at right angles to your planks (Fig. 2.), to measure for the 2 x 8 backing piece. Measure from edge to edge, then subtract 6 inches and cut your 2 x 8 to that length. Lay this backing piece across the upside-down tabletop. It should be 3 inches from each edge, centered from the outer edges. Hold the planks tightly together, then drill the pilot holes for the screws using four screws for each tabletop plank, spaced as shown in Fig. 2.

Do not move any of the planks while drilling the pilot holes. Hold the tabletop planks together too. Drill the countersink holes, then the screw-shank holes in the backing plank. Tighten all screws.

Make a pencil line along each of the six sides ¾ inches in from the edge. Cut the 1½ x 1½ pieces to length, parallel to the edges, behind the pencil mark. The ends will all be cut at 60-degree angles and will be adjacent to each other. Fasten these pieces with one screw about 1 inch from

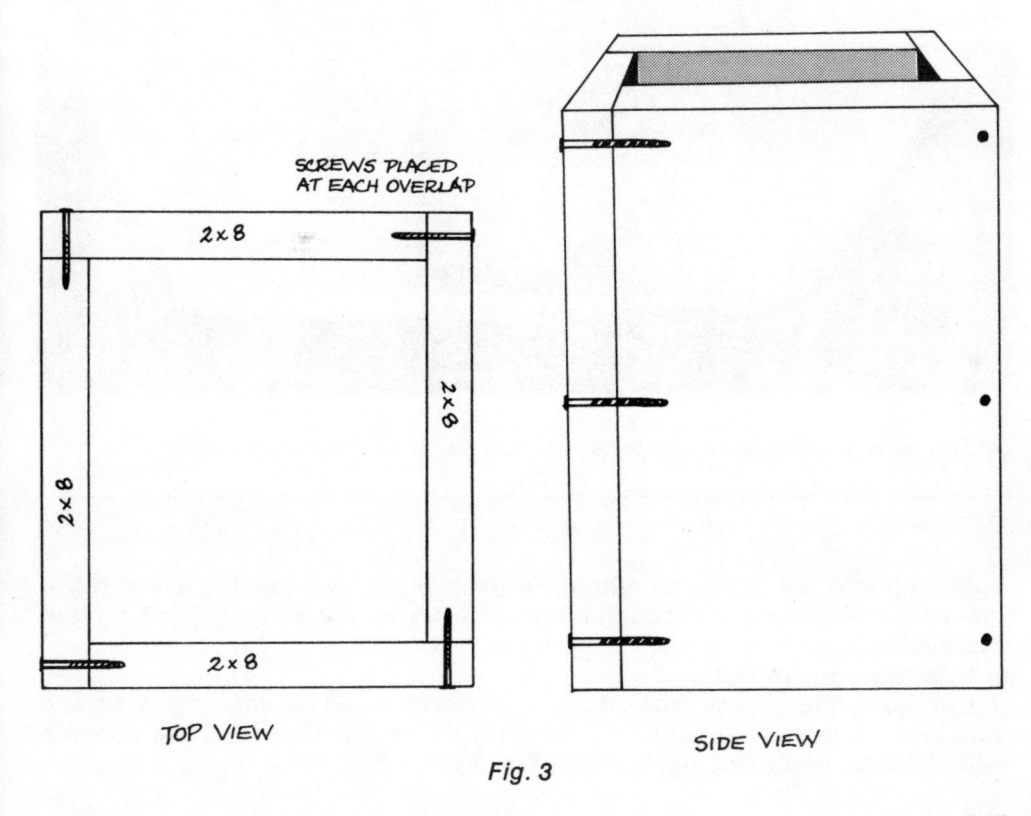

Fig. 3

Underside view of tabletop complete with backing plank and edge pieces.

each end and one screw centered on each plank that the 1½ x 1½ piece crosses. Drill your pilot, countersink, and screw shank holes and tighten the screws.

Now make the pedestal.

Cut 4 24-inch pieces from the 2 x 8. Form these pieces into a square with one edge overlapping. The ends must be flush and square. Secure with three screws along each edge. (Fig. 3.)

Pedestal complete.

Cut the legs from the 2 x 4 as shown in Fig. 4, using a carpenter's square. Align the carpenter's square on the 2 x 4 for the legs so that the short part reads 11 inches (on the outside scale of the square) to the 2 x 4 and the long side reads 16 inches (outside scale) to the 2 x 4.

Fasten the legs to the pedestal by setting the pedestal on something solid (a thick book, block of wood), raising it 2½ inches above the surface of a flat table, bench, or floor. The pedestal must stand perfectly straight.

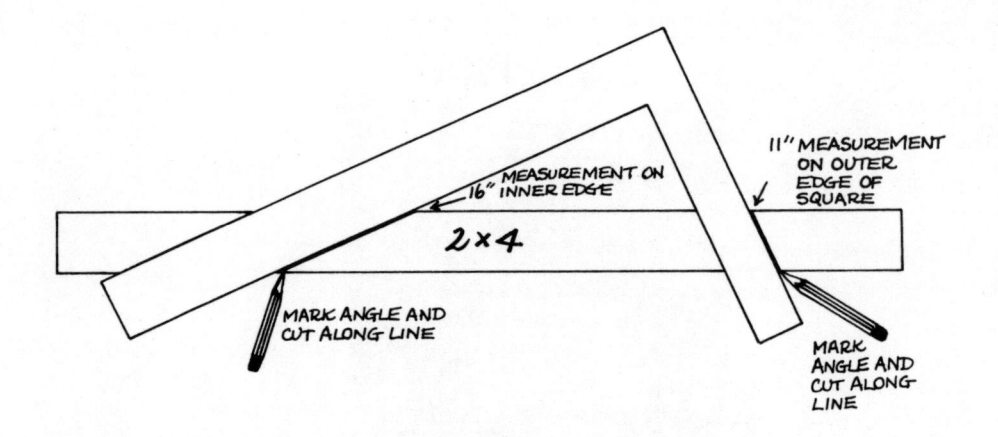

Fig. 4

You may want to clamp it to something. Take one of the legs and hold it against the flat of the pedestal with the long cut lying flat on the floor. (Fig. 5.)

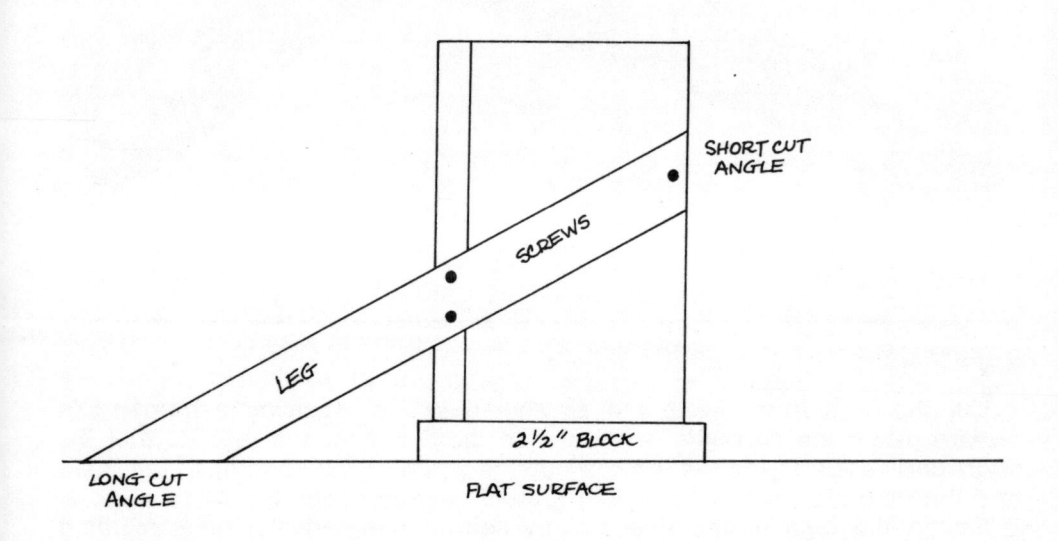

Fig. 5

Put one leg on each flat surface of the pedestal, working around it, until the legs are all attached as shown in Fig. 6.

Set your tabletop on the pedestal, with the backing piece for the top resting on the pedestal. Center the top.

Fasten one of the 3-inch angle braces on each side of the pedestal, centered on the pedestal and the backing piece. Notice that you can attach only two of the angle braces onto the backing piece.

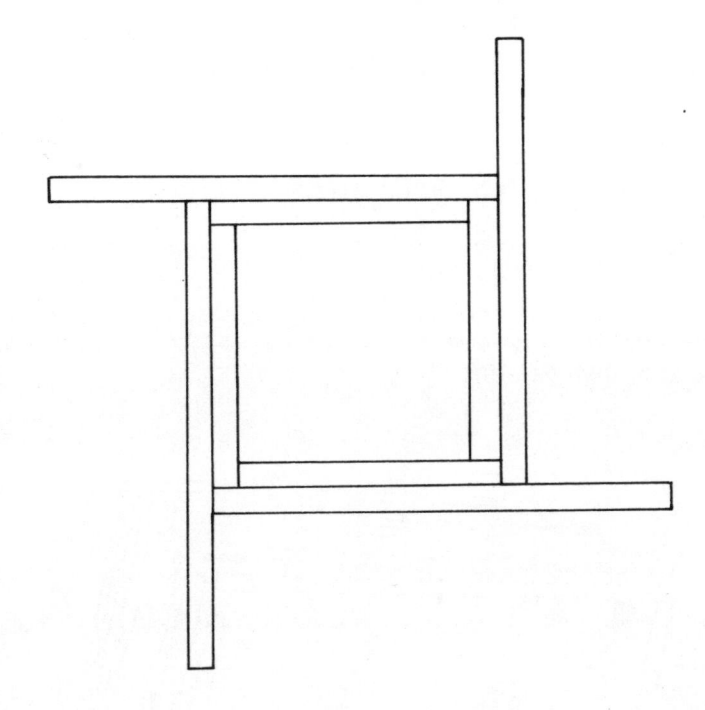

Fig. 6

To attach the other two angle braces to the top and the pedestal, take two scrap pieces of 2 x 4s (the long angle cuts) or some leftover 2 x 8s and fasten them with screws to the underside of the tabletop on either side of the pedestal. Then fasten the remaining two 3-inch corner braces to the pedestal and to the blocks.

CHAPTER 21

MORE USEFUL PLANS AND IDEAS

Basic outlines for a number of useful and attractive designs are assembled in this chapter. This is the idea section — I hope that it will inspire you to make your own designs.

Clutter Boxes

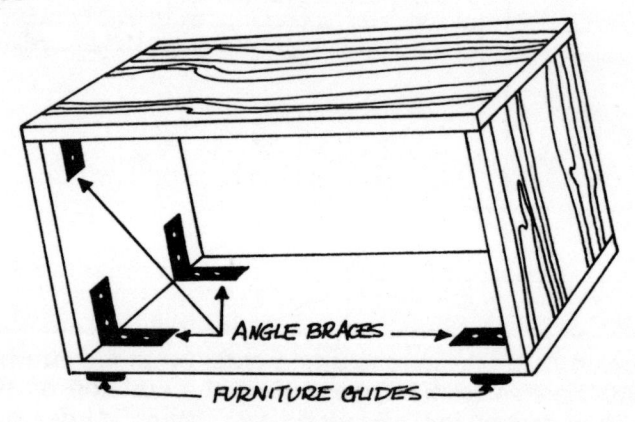

Fig. 1

Clutter boxes are always useful and these are decorative too.
Make your clutter box about 16 to 18 inches high and up to 40 inches long. This is a light-duty table — good for magazines and feet, but not for sitting.

Take four pieces of ¾-inch plywood, all the same width, and join them together with glue and 1-inch angle braces. The top and bottom should overlap the ends. (Fig. 1.) Line up the angle braces on the top and bottom, and screw in place — about ¾ inches in from each end and 2 inches in from the edge (widthwise), but screwed to the top piece only. Apply a liberal amount of wood glue to the leg piece, following directions on the can. Then, slide the ends into place, and attach the leg pieces to the angle braces. If you like, glue veneer taping to the edges, then finish.

Make sure that your cuts are straight, or the legs will be crooked. To decrease the wobble caused by uneven floors, get some furniture glides from your hardware store and put them under the corners.

Stand

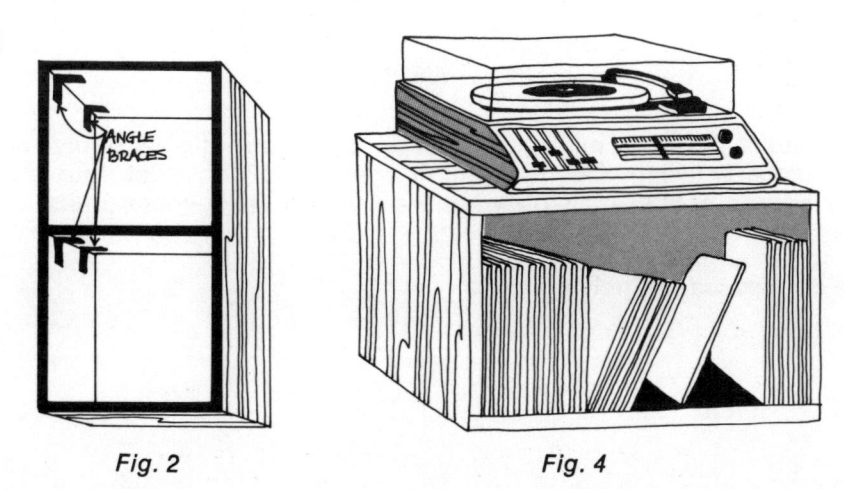

Fig. 2

Fig. 4

You can make a clutter box into a stand for the bedroom or bathroom simply by tipping it on end and adding a shelf below the top, using angle braces. (Fig. 2.)

Also, you can make an open cube, lay it on edge, put a top on it, and you have a **coffee table.** Attach the top with angle braces. (Fig. 3.) Or, use an open cube for a **stereo stand** with records underneath. (Fig. 4.)

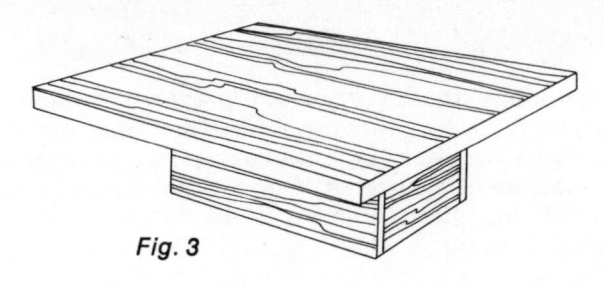

Fig. 3

Shelving Unit

Fig. 5

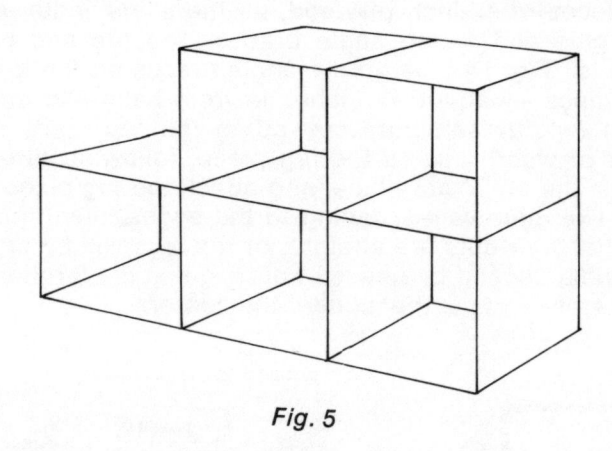

To extend the open cube idea further, cut square pieces of plywood and construct a shelving unit. It is much cheaper to construct your own with angle braces and ½-inch plywood than to buy ready-made units. (Fig. 5.)

More Bookcases or Shelving Units

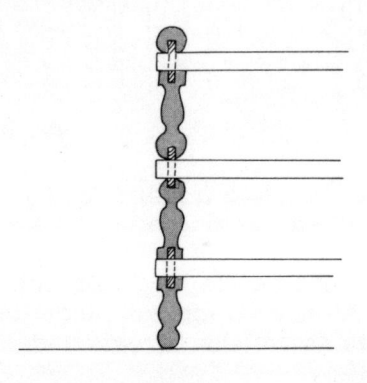

Fig. 6

Most building-supply stores carry wood pieces that have been turned on a lathe and can be joined by threaded dowels. These are ideal for making shelving units, room dividers, or bookcases. Buy boards or plywood the size that you need for the shelves. Get the right number of spacers and connectors. Drill holes through the shelves for the connecting threaded dowels. Assemble. (Fig. 6.)

Hammocks for Storage

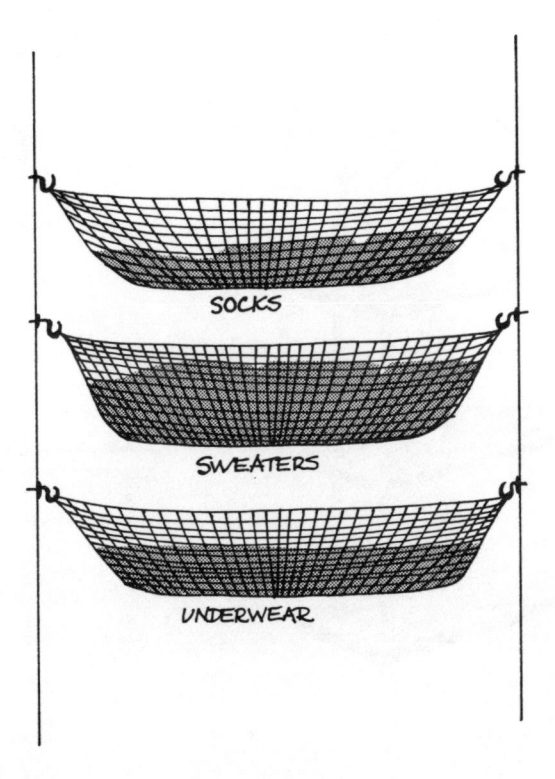

Fig. 7

Borrow an idea from the sailors and use netting for hammocks to store clothes, towels, and other household items. Every good sailor has netting over his bunk to hold items that he needs often. The advantage of using netting is that you can see through it. Thus you know instantly what is where.

Any light netting will do. It is available in small packs for wall decoration. Cut some pieces about 20 inches wide and about 36 inches long, or whatever size suits you. Experiment with some sizes before cutting.

Set some proportionately sized screw hooks into a wall or other upright surface. Hook the netting ends over it. The secret of a good netting bag is to hang the edges tighter (shorter) than the middle. Do this by dropping a few of the mesh openings on the edge lines of the netting.

Rope-Slung Shelves

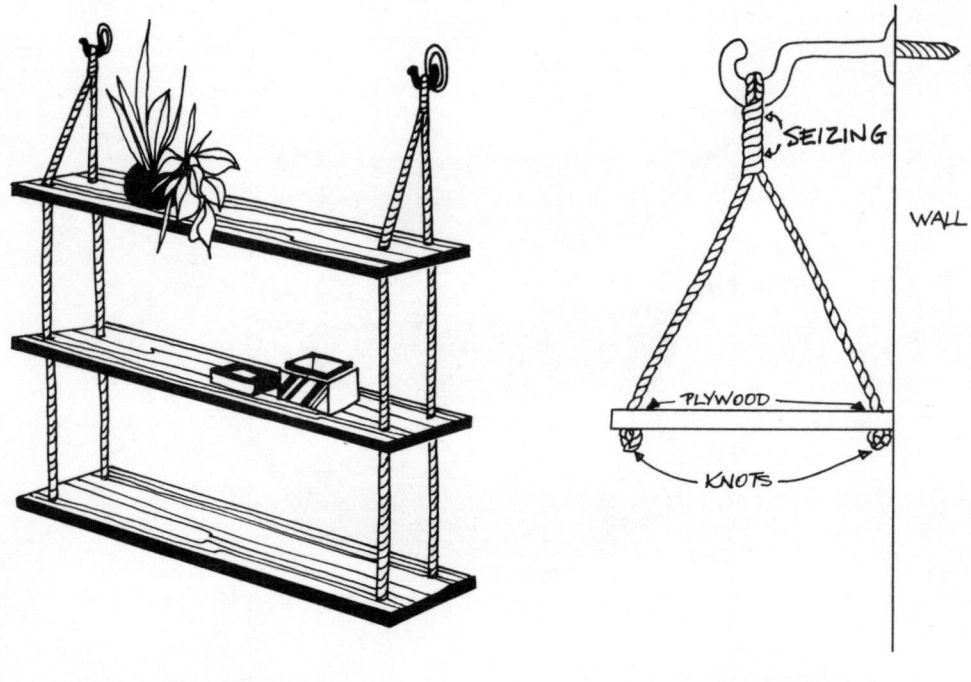

Fig. 8 *Fig. 9*

Extending the nautical idea a little further, hang (or gimbal in nautical terminology) boards with a rope to form shelves on a wall. Put some hooks into the wall to support the shelves. If you are going to put heavy things on the shelves, get some really sturdy hooks and make sure that they are anchored into wall studs.

Drill a hole near each corner of the board for the rope. Thread the ends of the rope through the boards and knot them. Hang the rope on the hooks. Level the shelf by adjusting the knots. Then put some seizing (light twine wrapped several times around the rope very tightly to prevent it from sliding around the hook). This is to make sure that the shelf will stay flat. You can hang several shelves one below the other, but each lower shelf will be harder to align because of the stretch of the rope and the different weights of the loads on the upper shelves.

The shelves should not be more than 15 inches wide, or more than 48 inches long. Any longer than that and they will sag. Use pine, plywood, whatever.

Collapsible Writing Table

Another nautical design that is very handy for apartment dwellers is the fold-down chart table (writing table for you landlubbers).

A good size is 28 x 20. Get a piece of plywood about this size. Half-inch plywood will do, but ¾-inch will make your table more solid. You also need two 2 x 2s about 12 inches long. Attach these to the wall 1 inch higher than where you want your writing surface. Leave a gap of about 3 inches between the 2 x 2 for the leg that swings away from the wall. You will need a 1 x 2 as a leg to hinge from the floor to support the table about 6 inches from the edge.

For a 28 x 20 table, attach two 2 x 2s, 35 inches above the floor, (Fig. 10.) Attach the plywood to the 2 x 2 with a pair of strap hinges.

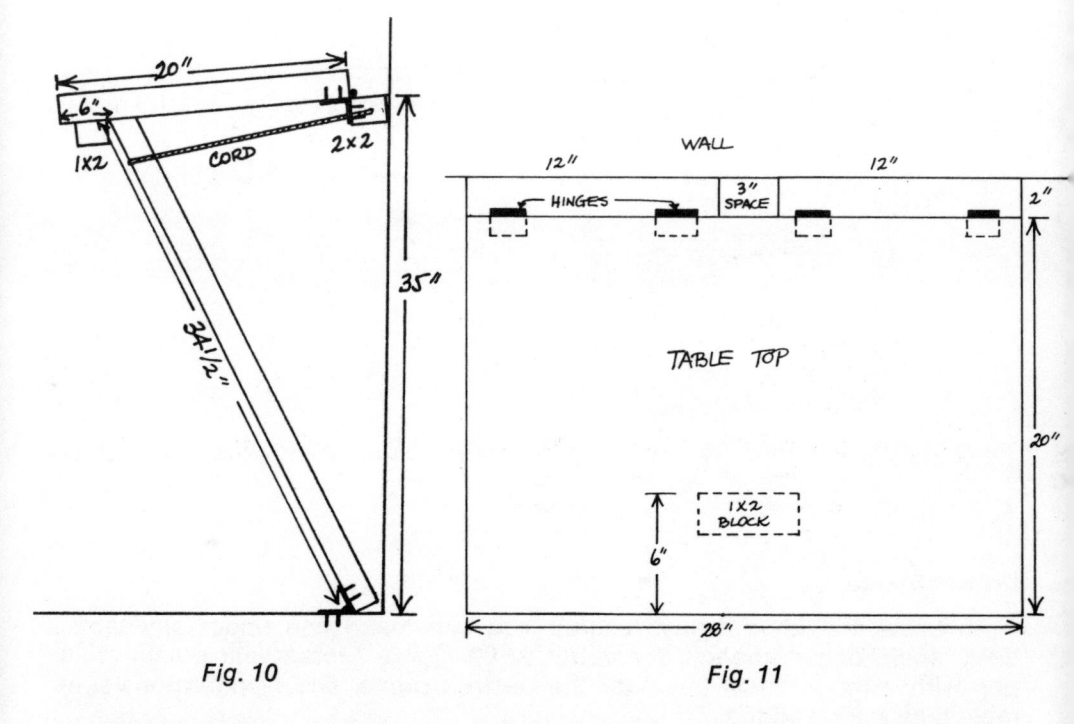

Fig. 10

Fig. 11

Cut a 1 x 2 34½ inches long and hinge it from the floor so that when the tabletop is down, it will hinge flat against the wall in the gap between the 2 x 2.

Attach a cord to loop around the 1 x 2 to keep it from falling too far from the wall. A 1 x 2 block tacked on to the plywood 6 inches from the edge to serve as a stopper block for the leg is also helpful.

More Seats, Benches, Tables

For something attractive to sit on, yet easy to make, cover old packing crates with a thick shag carpet (preferably carpet with foam backing).

Any wooden crates or pop cases will do. Even old television or stereo cabinets that have been gutted can be dressed up in this way. An old television cabinet might have to have a piece of plywood tacked across the front and bottom, the legs removed, and then laid on its back, but this is still easier than starting from scratch.

Cut the carpet to fit, as shown in Fig. 12 and tack it on with (what else?) carpet tacks.

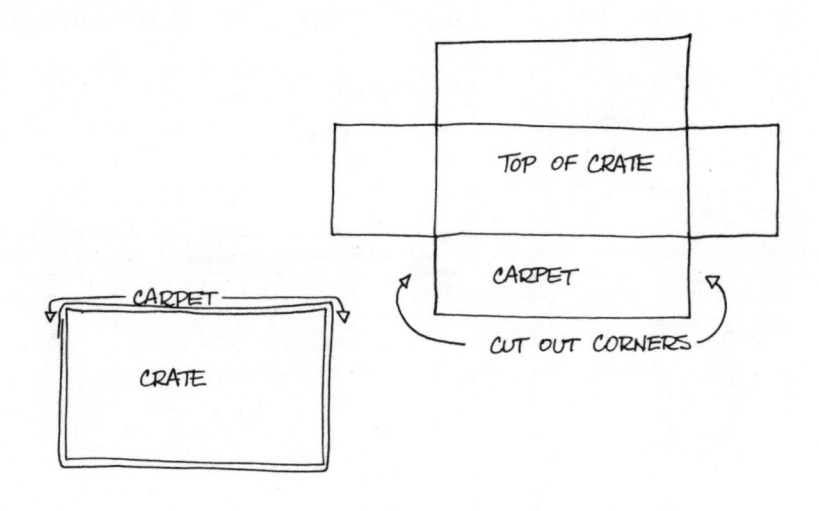

Fig. 12

Drawer Space

An extra drawer is always useful. You can make one under any table, desk, shelf, or workbench, for about $2.00. Get a rectangular plastic dish pan with a lip that will fit under the desired place. Old refrigerator vegetable bins work well too.

Get two 1 x 2 boards and two 1 x 3 boards that are the length (or slightly longer) than the dishpan. Nail and glue these in place as shown in Fig. 13. Cut a finger hole in the front of the pan to facilitate opening. Put a block behind the drawer to stop it from sliding too far back.

Note: Make sure that the 1 x 3 fits really close to the pan under the lip, or the pan might pop out when loaded.

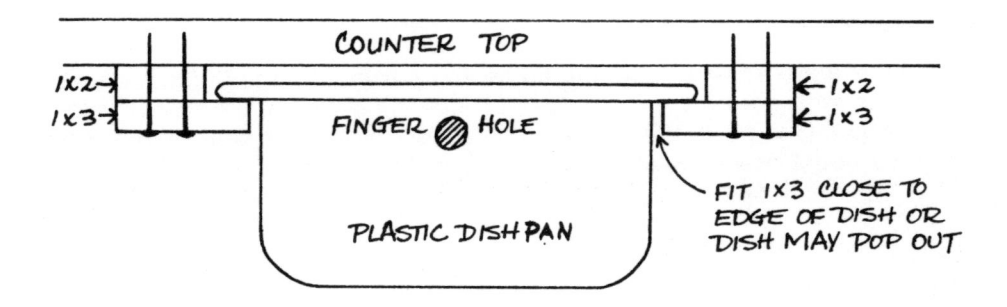

Fig. 13

The above drawers are for light-duty use. If you want to keep canned goods or heavy utensils in the pans, here is what you do instead:

Get some metal strapping from your hardware store, the kind with holes in it about every inch. It is sold in rolls.

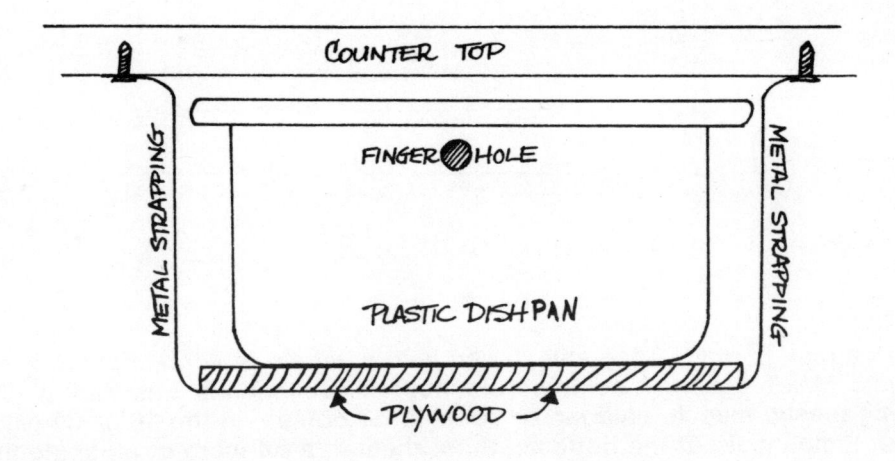

Fig. 14

Cut a piece of ¼-inch plywood, or whatever size you have on hand, just a bit bigger than the size of the plastic dishpan. Hang this plywood — with the dishpan sitting on it— with the metal strapping. Use a good stout screw at each end of the strap. (Fig. 14.)

Wine Rack

Need a wine rack or pigeon holes for sorting things? You can easily make one with some 2 x 2 or 1½-inch doweling and some ⅜-inch doweling. A regular wine bottle will fit into a 4-inch square and, with supports 9 inches apart, the cork end will be lower. (Fig. 15.)

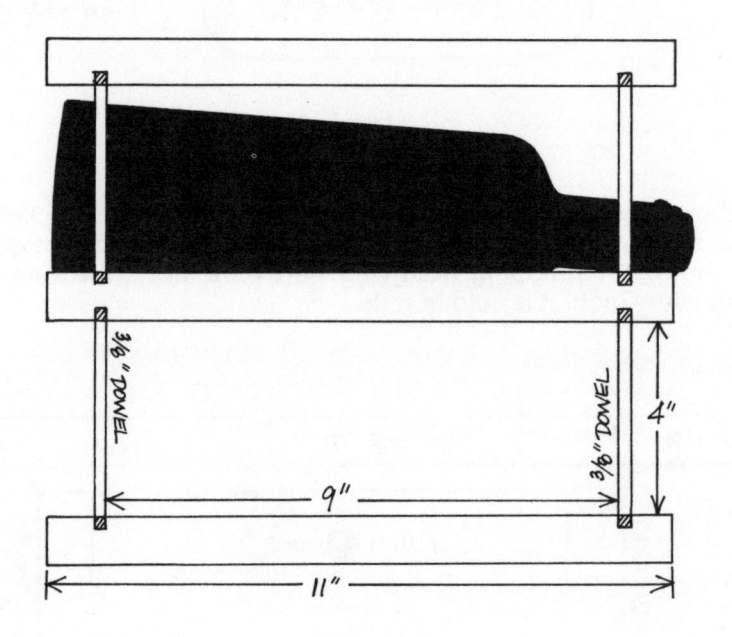

Fig. 15

This rack is really adaptable. It can hold a variety of kitchen or workshop items. Make a handy container to hold miscellaneous bits and pieces, using plastic bleach, vinegar, or cooking oil bottles, in the 16 or 20-ounce size. Simply cut out the bottoms. Store them at a bit more of an angle than the wine bottles by shortening the back dowel on the rack. This will prevent things from falling out.

To construct the rack, drill a ⅜-inch hole just less than half the thickness of your 2 x 2 or 1½-inch dowel. Drill four holes, all pointing toward the same point. (Fig. 16.)

Put the ⅜-inch dowels and the 2 x 2 together like an erector set. For more stability, glue the ⅜-inch dowels and 2 x 2 together. This will make it rigid, the disadvantage being that you will not be able to dismantle it.

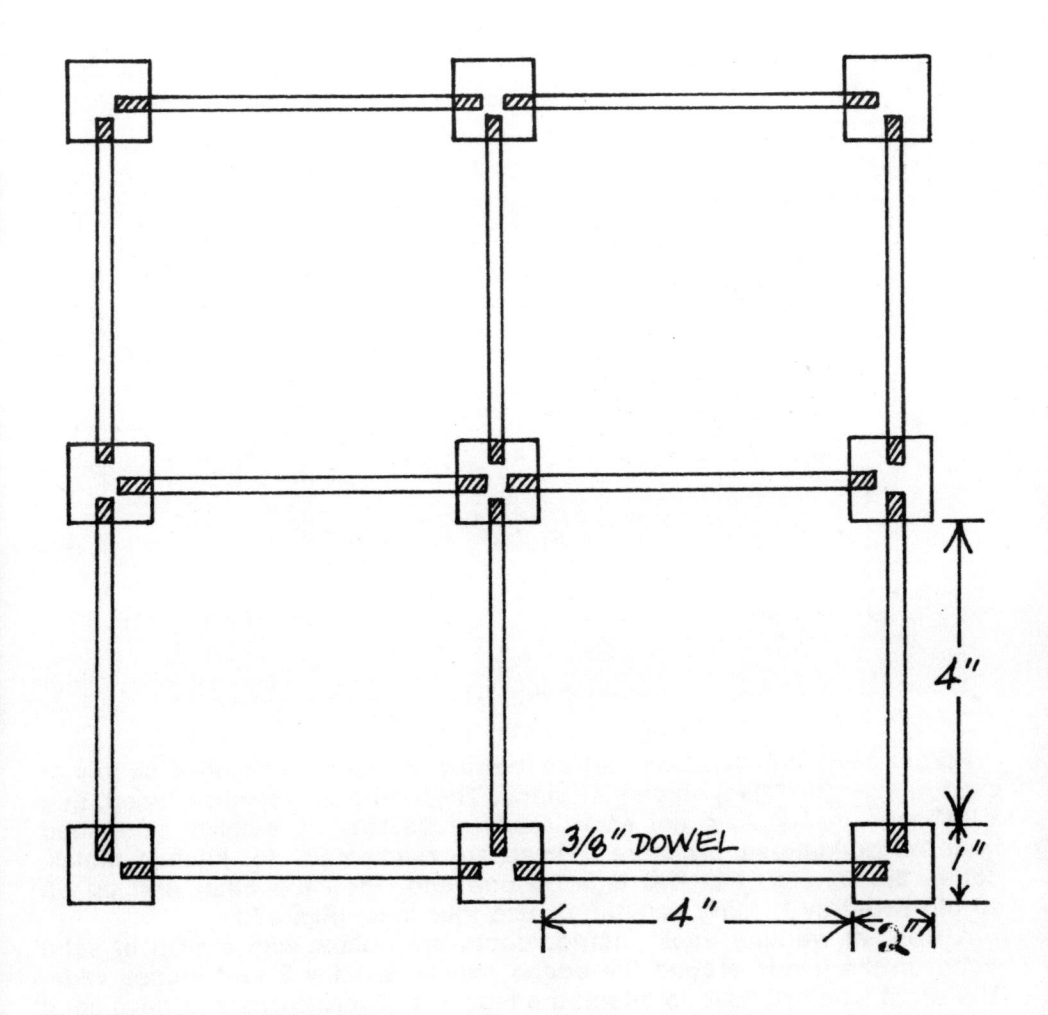

Fig. 16

Shelves on a Wall

The easiest way to install shelves on a wall is to use a shelf bracket. Buy these at a hardware store and simply set a board on them. Make sure that the bracket is solidly attached to the wall, or your shelf may come tumbling down.

159

Desk

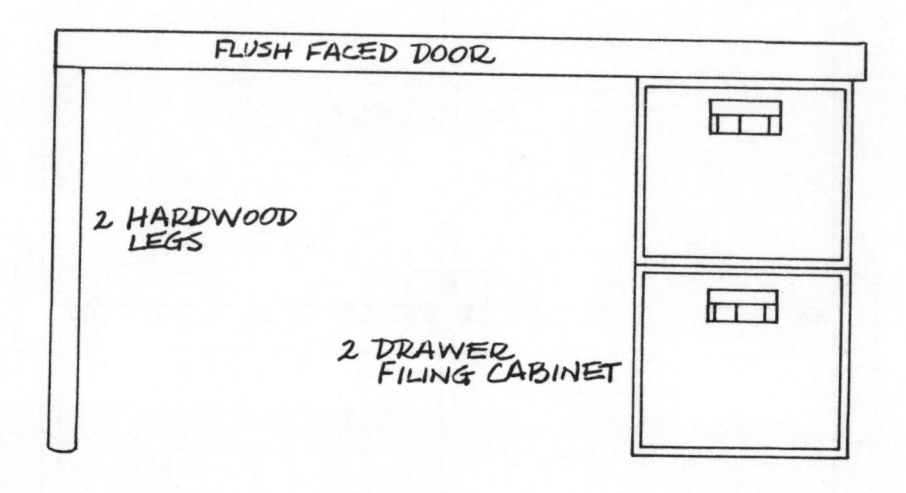

Fig. 17

For an easy-to-make desk, get an interior door from a building-supply or used lumber (building wrecker's) place. These are usually flush-faced, that is, with no insets. Also get some ready-made legs of metal or hardwood from the building-supply store. (These are ready-made for kitchen tables, coffee tables, etc.) Put two legs on one end. Prop the other end up on an old two-drawer filing cabinet, or use four legs. (Fig. 17.)

A word of warning: most interior doors are hollow with a strip of solid wood on the inside around the edges only — usually 2 to 4 inches wide. Therefore, you will have to attach the legs at the very corners to have solid backing for your screws. Or, you can attach the legs to a board, then the door to the board.

If you do not want to spend the money on furniture legs, go to a hardware store, get pipe stands and a piece of pipe the correct length and diameter, and use these instead. Put a rubber chair-leg tip on the end of the pipe to protect your floor.